ALL NATURAL
MUSCULAR
Development

Presents

MUSCLE MEALS

MUSCLE MEALS

By John Romano

For information contact: Advanced Research Press, 2120 Smithtown Avenue, Ronkonkoma, NY 11779.

FIRST EDITION

Library of Congress Cataloging-in-Publication Data

John Romano

Muscle Meals

1. Cooking 2. Physical Fitness 3. Health

1. Title

Library of Congress Catalog Number 97-71088

ISBN 1-889462-01-2

Printed in the United States of America.

Published by: Advanced Research Press, Inc.
                                 2120 Smithtown Avenue
                                 Ronkonkoma, NY 11779

Publisher/President: Steve Blechman
Project Director: Roy Ulin
Art Directors: Ed Passarelli
                                 Marc Passarelli

Copy Editor: Jessica Richmond
Cover Photography: Ken Marcus
Illustrator: Lyman Dally
Printed by: R.R. Donnelley & Sons

This book is dedicated to my two little

angels, Kristine and Danielle: all of the

sunshine a man could ever need. And to

my wife Shelley, who proves to me every

day that reality can exceed my dreams.

ABOUT THE AUTHOR

John Romano is an accomplished bodybuilder and trainer of top athletes who first gained notoriety as "the Muscle Chef" when he started dishing out out culinary advise to bodybuilders and fitness buffs at Gold's Gym in Venice, California. As most bodybuilding and fitness devotees know, this gym is known as the "Mecca of Bodybuilding" because of the bodybuilding champions, professional athletes, fitness stars, and Hollywood celebrities who regularly train there.

It was at Gold's Gym where John began to amass a clientele of bodybuilding and fitness stars eager to apply his expertise to their contest preparation. One of his charges had John accompany her to Columbus Ohio in 1992 for her competitive outing in Arnold Schwarzenegger's Ms. International competition. This is where he met his wife Shelley Beattie. Under John's tutelage Shelley became one of the best women bodybuilders in the world, placing 3rd in Joe Weider's 1992 Ms. Olympia. She went on, with John's help, to become a star on TV's American Gladiators, known to millions as Siren on the popular show, and then subsequently John helped Shelley secure a spot on America Cubed; the prestigious, first in its history, all women Americas Cup sailing team.

John's lineage includes a long line of culinary experts including his father; an expert bread baker by hobby, his mother; who owns and operates a gourmet bakery, his sister; a pastry chef, and his brother; who has cheffed at high end restaurants in New York, California, Vermont and Virginia. Through their influences and that of the great chefs John worked with in some of the country's best restaurants, he contemplated attending the prestigious Culinary Institute of America and perusing a career as a professional chef. In the end he opted to peruse a career as a bodybuilder, trainer and writer. But his penchant for cooking remained in the forefront of his professional endeavors and his reputation grew throughout the bodybuilding community for his ability to prepare great tasting meals within the caloric, nutritional and low-fat guidelines needed by bodybuilders and fitness competitors. Subsequently, John was invited to be the bodybuilding chef on ESPN's popular TV magazine, American Muscle, where his segment, Muscle Meals, became an instant success.

John then became a cooking and nutritional consultant to Twin Laboratories, Inc., the nation's leading manufacturer of sports supplements. Twinlab asked John to develop a series of low fat, high protein recipes using a new all vegetable protein supplement Twinlab had developed called Vege Fuel. Vege Fuel uses 100% pure soy protein isolate as its protein source. This presented a culinary challenge which John couldn't resist. A number of these Vege Fuel fortified recipes appear in this book as well as in the Vege Fuel Cookbook which accompanies the product.

John also became a regular contributor to Muscular Development Magazine, with a monthly column aptly entitled Muscle Meals. So many bodybuilding and fitness devotees wrote to John asking for his culinary advise that he decided to write this book. It is written in the humorous style that is Romano and is illustrated by the world's greatest bodybuilding cartoonist, Lyman Dally. We know you'll enjoy the reading, the illustrations, and the Muscle Meals. But, most of all, in several months of enjoying your personal Muscle Meals menu, you'll enjoy a more muscular and leaner you.

Bon Appetite.

The Editorial Staff of
All Natural Muscular Development Magazine.

"I recommend *Muscle Meals* for any bodybuilder who wants to feed their muscles without insulting their palate."

Lee Labrada
Champion Bodybuilder

TABLE OF CONTENTS

Introduction

Congratulations on an excellent investment! You have just taken the first step toward satisfying the nutritional demands of bodybuilding and fitness with meals you are sure to enjoy. After reading this book, your diet will be transformed from blah and mundane to delicious and exciting.

Nutrition plays a vital role in how you look and feel; 80 percent of your training success depends on your diet. Food is fuel——nothing more, nothing less. The hard-core bodybuilder can build freakish amounts of muscle, or the fitness enthusiast can vastly improve performance, simply by implementing a nutritional strategy that fuels the body for growth and repair while keeping body fat levels low.

It takes a quantum degree of almost inhuman willpower to thrash your body to its limits in the gym day after day. Should dry, broiled chicken breasts and plain baked potatoes be your only reward? It's no wonder that most athletes get discouraged before they achieve the coveted status of champion.

Many athletes come to me for help because they have reached the nutritional equivalent of an immovable block. They have stopped improving because they can't force down another can of dry, flavorless tuna. Their efforts and determination, though admirable, have proved fruitless. The fortitude they exhibit in abstaining from culinary enjoyment ultimately robs their bodies of the essential fuel it needs to grow.

Regardless of the degree to which you'd like your body to develop—— competitive bodybuilder, fitness star, Adonis——you must adequately fuel your body. In other words, you have to eat right!

Muscle Meals are designed to fortify your body with the high-quality protein and complex carbohydrates it needs, while rewarding you with a delicious array of easy-to-prepare gourmet foods that you'll look forward to day after day. The result is a variety of low-fat treats that deliver the right nutrients and are easy to integrate into your bodybuilding or fitness lifestyle. In addition, if you go off the deep end and find yourself face-down in a Reese's-Peanut-Butter-Cup-chocolate-chip-cookie-dough-hot fudge-cheesecake-sundae, on the verge of an insulin-induced coma, you can relax. You'll find it much easier to return to a Muscle Meals menu of Chicken Cacciatori, Pasta with Zucchini and Mushrooms, and Espresso Custard than your usual dry, ground turkey patty and plain rice.

So keep reading! Freedom from nutritional boredom is within your grasp. This book was written with the novice cook in mind; all you need to be able to do is find the kitchen. Once Muscle Meals become a part of your lifestyle, you'll never go back to those ho-hum days of dry, tasteless food. With the energy from Muscle Meals' nutritious foods, you'll have the motivation to train consistently for the body of your dreams.

Living in Venice, California and training at the Mecca of bodybuilding, Gold's Gym, I've seen some of the world's most dedicated and hard-training athletes. These athletes know that dedication doesn't end in the gym, but must be maintained for pre-contest dieting and year-round nutritional maintenance.

I've been amazed that some of these people can eat the same bland, boring food day after day and never falter. These athletes succeed in bringing their body fat to ridiculously low levels——and keep it there. But spend time around some of them when a contest is approaching and you take your life into your hands! Observing this, I wondered if the same results couldn't be achieved by eating a creative yet carefully controlled diet that wouldn't leave you feeling bored, short-tempered, and resentful. So I put my culinary know-how to work.

Using what I'd learned over the years to make my own diet more enjoyable (and using myself as a guinea pig), I developed recipes that will support muscular gains and keep you interested in eating. During just 8 weeks of Muscle Meals dieting, I whittled my body fat down to a minuscule 3 percent while enjoying great tasting entrées and fabulous desserts. The bottom line is: Muscle Meals will help you gain muscle mass, lose body fat, improve performance, and maintain a top physique year-round.

The recipes I demonstrate on ESPN's American Muscle and those detailed in this book are excellent examples of the exciting food you can eat while scrupulously monitoring calories, carbohydrates, protein, and fat. With Muscle Meals, you won't feel as if you're missing out on anything. Try it! The results will speak for themselves.

Each Muscle Meals recipe contains complete nutritional information, so keeping track of your daily calorie, carbohydrate, protein, and fat totals is easy and foolproof. You are about to have your cake and eat it too!

Chapter One

MUSCLE MEALS IN THE MAKING

Your Kitchen

Because certain utensils are integral to Muscle Meal cooking, you may need to stock your kitchen with additional cooking equipment. This chapter contains a complete list of everything you'll need. Although you probably already have many of these items, you can make do with substitutes in some cases. However, using the proper utensils will make preparation easier and produce the best results.

Cookware

Stock pot, 12 to 20 quart: Stock pots can be found in gourmet shops, department stores, and restaurant supply stores. Beware of cheap, thin-bottomed pots. A well-made, thick-bottomed pot is your best insurance against a burned, encrusted coating on the bottom of the pot after long periods of cooking over high heat.

Sauté pan, 6-inch to 14-inch: A good quality, stainless-steel-lined pan is best. I like Al-Clad Ltd. brand pans, which are expensive but worth the price. The size of the pan you'll need is determined by the number of servings you'll be making at one time. I recommend that you purchase 1 small and 1 large.

Non-stick sauté pan, 6-inch to 14-inch: This is the same kind of pan described above, but coated with "Silver Stone" or "Never Stick". Buy a good quality, long-lasting pan, and only use wood or plastic utensils with it. Metal will scratch the pan and ruin the coating in no time flat.

Saucepans, 2-quart and 8-quart: Again, heavy pans lined with stainless steel are the best. Al-Clad gets my vote again.

Large roasting pan: Find the biggest one that will fit in your oven. A good, sturdy roasting pan has deep sides, a foldable handle on each end, and costs a small fortune. A used pan from the restaurant supply store is your best bet. I like the worn, black, ugly ones because they tend not to warp in the oven and are usually well-seasoned from years of use. In this case, looks don't count.

Sheet pans: Large aluminum sheet pans are so versatile that I keep 5 or 6 of them around for a variety of uses. Again, restaurant supply stores are the best source for inexpensive used sheet pans. Before you buy, make sure the pan will fit in your oven. For non-stick sheet pans, Ecko's fairly inexpensive pans are a good choice.

Cake pans: With two 9-inch round, two 9-inch square, and two 9- by

13-inch rectangular pans, you'll have everything you need. Ecko makes the best and most affordable non-stick pans. You can find them in your supermarket or discount store.

Muffin pans: Three 6-muffin pans will accommodate all of the batter any Muscle Meal recipe makes. Ecko gets my vote again.

Cheesecake pan, 9-inch: The best cheesecake pans have deep sides and a removable bottom. Good-quality cheesecake pans are made of aluminum and can be found in most kitchen and gourmet shops.

Loaf Pans: Look for Ecko in the supermarket or discount store. Three loaf pans will make enough Muscle Meals bread for your whole family.

Fire-proof bricks: Buy enough 1-inch-thick fire-proof bricks from your local building supply store to line the bottom rack of your oven. They are absolutely the best surface for cooking pizza and bread.

Wooden pizza peel: Found in kitchen and gourmet shops, a wooden pizza peel is the best utensil to remove bread and pizza from the oven. With this tool, you don't need to add fat to your recipes to prevent sticking.

Ramekins: Buy at least 6 or 8 Pyrex or ceramic 4-ounce ramekins at a kitchen or gourmet shop. Even if you never cook in them, they're great for holding ingredients while you're preparing a meal.

U t e n s i l s

Cutlery: I am religiously committed to Wüstoff Trident Cutlery. I have tried all of the high-end cutlery, and Wüstoff Trident is definitely the best. It is also one of the most expensive. Don't spend the money for a pre-packaged set; you won't need all of the cutlery it contains. One 6-inch or 8-inch chef's knife, one long slicing knife, and one boning knife should be all you need. In 15 years of cooking, I've never needed any other knives. If you buy the good stuff, you'll be glad you did.

Advice on sharpening: Some people send their knives out, some use a sharpening stone and honing steel, and others use electric sharpeners. I can proudly say that I've never had a knife leave my kitchen for sharpening. As for electric sharpeners, for a long time it was my opinion that they weren't good for anything except perhaps as wedding gifts for the bride who has everything. For years I stayed true to the stone and the steel. However, Chef's Choice now makes an electric sharpener that will render your knives razor-sharp in less time than it takes to dig the stone out of the drawer. Needless to say, I'm a convert.

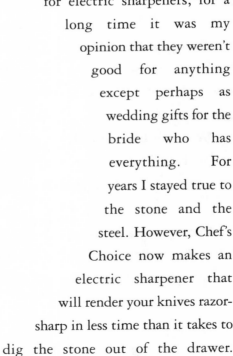

Wooden spoons: These are invaluable. Buy 3 good hardwood ones in various sizes at a kitchen or gourmet shop. Keep a very light coating of cooking oil on all of your wooden utensils to prevent them from drying out and splitting. Of course, you should never put them in the dishwasher.

Tongs: Buy 2 pairs; 1 small and 1 large. Any kind will do.

Rolling pin: I like the solid, 1-piece French type made of hardwood. Any high school student can make a great one for you in shop class (I still have the one I made), or you can pick up one at a kitchen or gourmet shop.

Rubber spatula: Rubbermaid makes the best. They are not heat-proof, but they last the longest. Buy 3 large ones and 3 small ones.

Metal spatula: This doesn't have to be a Wüstoff Trident, although they do look nice. Any restaurant-quality, stainless steel spatula will do.

Pastry brush: Ecko wins again.

Wire whisk: I use mine at least twice a day. Get a both a small and a large one from a kitchen or gourmet shop.

Sieve/Colander: Buy a plastic one for draining and a metal one for steaming.

Strainers: Buy one 6-inch and one 10-inch. Ecko is the best.

Measuring cups and spoons: I own 1- and 2-cup Pyrex measuring cups and some nondescript plastic spoon measures. The supermarket can probably supply everything you'll need.

Cutting board: I like the white plastic boards from the restaurant supply store. They won't stain or chip and are quite inexpensive. Also, unlike wooden boards, plastic can be sterilized easily, which is important when working with raw poultry. Cutting space is always at a premium, so buy the biggest cutting board your work space can accommodate.

Mixing bowls: 2 small, 2 medium, and 2 large stainless steel mixing bowls should hold just about anything you prepare. Discount stores often carry these in multi-size sets. I prefer the heavier, kitchen store variety.

Food processor: A food processor is not mandatory, but will certainly save you time. I like the miniature ones because they are easier to use and clean, and are more powerful than the larger Cuisinart types.

Electric mixer: This is another optional luxury. I own a professional quality Kitchen Aid. I use it constantly, for everything from kneading dough to beating egg whites. Once you use one, you'll never go back to mixing by hand.

The items listed above are to what I've been able to reduce my kitchen tool supply, and still be able to produce great food. I still own a bunch of special purpose stuff that I rarely use but is nice to have if the occasion arises. Even the most pared-down version of a well-equipped kitchen can cost a small fortune. Take your time. Opportunities to stock up will present themselves: Friends and family relocate, restaurants go out of business, and neighbors have garage sales. Don't wait to start cooking until you own all of the tools I've mentioned. Do the best you can with what you've got and buy new tools as needed.

Techniques and Terms

Al dente: Literally, "to the teeth", this term is used to describe cooked grains that are tender, yet firm in the center. Most of the pasta and rice used in Muscle Meals recipes will be cooked until al dente.

Boning: I can't say enough about boning. Although some people who watch me leave meat on bones scream that I'm wasting it, it's my opinion that it's not what stays on the bone that counts, but what's taken off. I like my fillets to be clean and uniform, free of tendons and cartilage. If I leave some meat on the bone, I don't worry because I always make my own stock. There is never any waste in my kitchen!

Butterflying: Butterflying is a technique for flattening out a piece of meat or fish. To butterfly, cut around the bone with a boning knife and remove it. Lay the meat smooth side down and cut into either side from where the bone used to be, with the knife parallel to the cutting surface. Stop before you reach the ends, creating two flaps. Turn the meat over, peel the flaps back, and pound flat with a mallet or the side of a can. Inspect the meat again and remove any newly exposed fat. When you are done, the two flaps of meat winging out from the line where the bone used to be are supposed to look like a butterfly.

Chopping: To chop is to cut into uniform 1/4- to 1/2-inch pieces.

Folding: Egg whites must be folded gently into the other ingredients. Because beaten egg whites are filled with air bubbles, you must take care not to deflate them when you introduce them into the heavier mixture. To fold egg whites, add 1/4 of the whites to your batter and mix well to loosen the mixture. Add the remaining egg whites and gently cut down through the mixture until the spatula hits the bottom of the bowl. Turn the spatula 1/4 turn as you scrape the bottom of the bowl, then lift the contents up with the broad side of the spatula until the batter breaks the surface of the egg whites. Start turning the spatula another 1/4 turn, completing the motion as the spatula comes to the surface. Repeat this process just until all of the egg whites are incorporated——try not to overfold. Save all of the air bubbles you can!

Mincing: Mincing produces much finer pieces than chopping. A minced ingredient should barely be visible in the finished dish. You most commonly will mince garlic and aromatic herbs.

Sautéing: When sautéing, use your stove's highest setting and keep the food moving to prevent it from burning. When you sauté vegetables, especially onions, use slightly less heat and add a small amount of salt (1/2 to 1 teaspoon) to help extract the water trapped in the vegetables. The high heat helps to evaporate the liquid and concentrate the flavor. Because sliced meats cook rapidly, you must take care not to overcook them. Even if you coat the pan with cooking spray, the liquid rendered from the food will caramelize and stick to the bottom of the pan. It is important to monitor the heat to keep this coating from burning.

Note: Non-stick pans don't fare well in extended high-heat conditions. Do most of your sautéing in uncoated pans. Whatever sticks to the pan will be taken care of when the pan is "deglazed".

Deglazing: During deglazing, the food particles and juices that have caramelized at the bottom of the pan are loosened and dissolved in liquid (usually stock). Deglazing can be done in an empty pan or a full one. After adding the stock, use a wooden spoon to scrape the pan. Once the pan is deglazed, you will "reduce" the liquid.

Reducing: Reducing is a method of concentrating the flavor of a dish by evaporating some or all of the water. To reduce something "by half" is to boil away half of the liquid, thus doubling the flavor concentration.

Water bath: A water bath is a method of cooking the contents of one pan with the heat from the boiling water in another. It ensures that the food cooks slowly and evenly. To make a water bath, cover the first pan with aluminum foil and set it in a larger and deeper pan (the bottom part of the broiling pan that came with your oven works best). Place the bigger pan on the extended center rack of the oven and fill with boiling water to within 1/2 inch of the top. Slide the rack back into the oven and gently shut the door.

By the way, dried herbs can be substituted for fresh in any of the Muscle Meals recipes. They won't taste as good, but they are more convenient to store. For each 1/2 cup of fresh herbs, you can substitute 2 teaspoons of dried herbs.

C h a p t e r   T w o

SOUPS AND SALADS

S o u p   S t o c k

Stock is possibly the most frequently used ingredient in Muscle Meals recipes. Stock isn't only for soup; it is also very useful in sauces, gravies, and stews.

Stock preparation seems time consuming but it really isn't. Once the ingredients are in the pot, it's a "no brainer". Remember, you don't have to tend the stock while it cooks——you can go work out or do your aerobics while it slowly bubbles away on its own.

I recommend that you spend 20 to 50 dollars and buy a 12-quart stock pot at any major department store. Although gourmet shops have slightly better quality pots, they sell them at tremendously higher prices. Alternatively, a used 15- to 20-quart aluminum or stainless-steel-lined stock pot from a restaurant supply store won't set you back too much and will allow you to make enough of each kind of stock to last a month or more (it can be kept for quite some time in the freezer).

Of course, you can buy canned stock and avoid this whole section altogether. I know that today's busy lifestyles may preclude indulgences like making fresh, wholesome, economical soup stocks. However, if you set aside just one afternoon a month, I promise that you can keep that metallic taste out of your cooking and get your iron from better sources. The choice is yours.

Making stock is foolproof. The most important thing to remember is to remove the fat. The only way to remove all of it is to refrigerate the stock overnight. The fat will rise to the top and solidify, making it quite easy to remove and dispose of.

Stock will last up to 1 week in the refrigerator or up to 1 year in the freezer. It's best to freeze stock in Ziplock bags in 1- or 2-cup portions. If you have prepared the stock properly it will come out of the refrigerator with the consistency of loose Jell-O, which makes it very easy to bag. When you need stock, just take a bag out of the freezer and soak it in hot water to thaw. Yes, opening a can is easier, but this way you know exactly what you're eating. Believe me, you can taste the difference.

A Word about Soup

Stock is the foundation of any soup. The few recipes you'll find on the following pages represent just a fraction of what you can do. Use your imagination! You can create hundreds of different soups by adding just about anything to the stock.

Beef Stock

5 lbs beef bones

2 onions, peeled and halved

12 peppercorns

2 carrots, peeled and cut into 3 pieces

10 whole cloves

3 bay leaves

3 stalks celery

1 head garlic, cut in half crosswise

3 sprigs parsley

Preheat the oven to 400°F. Place the bones in a roasting pan and bake them, turning occasionally, until they turn brown.

Transfer the browned bones to a stock pot and add the remaining ingredients. Add enough water to the pot to cover the ingredients by 2 inches. Bring to a boil, then lower the heat until the stock bubbles slightly. Simmer for 4 hours, skimming the froth off the top.

Turn off the heat and let the stock cool for about 1 hour, until tepid. Strain through a cheesecloth-lined sieve into a smaller saucepan. Discard the contents of the sieve.

Bring the stock to a rolling boil and reduce by half. Remove from the heat, let cool, and refrigerate overnight. The fat will have solidified on the top, and should be easy to remove and dispose of. Store the stock in 1- and 2-cup portions in Ziplock bags in the freezer.

Servings	Calories	Protein	Carbohydrates	Fat
6	34	1 g	6 g	0 g

Fish Stock

2 lbs bones and trimmings from whitefish

2 onions

3 sprigs parsley

juice of 2 lemons

2 tsp salt

1 cup white wine

10 cups water

Combine the ingredients in a stock pot. Bring to a boil, then lower the heat until the stock bubbles slightly. Simmer for 4 hours, skimming off the froth as it rises to the top. Turn off the heat and let the stock cool for about 1 hour, until tepid. Strain through a cheesecloth-lined sieve into a smaller saucepan. Discard the contents of the sieve.

Bring the stock to a rolling boil and reduce by half. Remove from the heat, let cool, and refrigerate overnight. The fat will have risen to the top and solidified, and should be easy to remove and dispose of. Store the stock in 1- and 2-cup portions in Ziplock bags in the freezer.

Servings	Calories	Protein	Carbohydrates	Fat
6	42	0 g	4 g	0 g

Chicken Stock

2 lbs chicken backs and necks

1 onion, quartered

1 carrot, cut in thirds

3 celery ribs and leaves, cut in thirds

1 head garlic, split crosswise in half

2 bay leaves

12 pepper corns

12 sprigs parsley

2 sprigs fresh basil

2 quarts water

Place the chicken pieces at the bottom of a large stock pot. Add the remaining ingredients and enough water to cover them by at least 2 inches. Simmer for 4 hours, skimming off the froth as it rises to the top. Turn off the heat and let the stock cool for about 1 hour, until tepid. Strain through a cheesecloth-lined sieve into a smaller saucepan. Discard the contents of the sieve.

Bring the stock to a rolling boil and reduce by half. Remove from the heat, let cool, and refrigerate overnight. The fat will have risen to the top and solidified, and should be easy to remove and dispose of. Store the stock in 1- and 2- cup portions in Ziplock bags in the freezer.

Servings	Calories	Protein	Carbohydrates	Fat
6	24	1 g	5 g	0 g

Chicken Noodle Soup

2 oz pasta
2 cups chicken stock
salt and pepper

Cook the pasta in 1 quart of lightly salted boiling water until al dente. Drain and set aside.

Bring the stock to a boil. Add the pasta and season to taste with salt and pepper.

For variety, carrots, celery, and onions can be added to the boiling stock and cooked until tender. Add the pasta last.

Servings	Calories	Protein	Carbohydrates	Fat
1	234	8 g	47 g	1 g

Cioppino

6 cups fish stock

1 can whole tomatoes, chopped and drained

1/4 tsp saffron threads, crushed into a powder

4 large shrimp, peeled and deveined

6 clams, scrubbed clean

6 mussels, scrubbed clean and de-bearded (see page 163)

4 oz haddock fillet, cut into chunks

1 potato, peeled and cut into chunks

1/2 cup white wine

1 onion, chopped

1 bay leaf

olive-oil-flavored cooking spray

1/4 cup fresh parsley, finely chopped

2 Tbs lemon juice

salt and pepper

Coat the surface of a large saucepan with olive-oil-flavored cooking spray. Sauté the onion until just brown. Add the white wine, bay leaf, potato, tomatoes, stock, and saffron, and bring to a boil. Reduce the heat and simmer for 30 to 40 minutes, until the potatoes are tender. Raise the heat and return to a boil. Add all of the seafood. Cover and cook for 5 to 10 minutes, until the shells open. Discard any shells that do not open. Add the parsley and lemon juice. Season with salt and pepper to taste. Stir and let stand for 15 minutes before serving.

Servings	Calories	Protein	Carbohydrates	Fat
4	183	17 g	23 g	1 g

Vegetable Beef Soup

8 pieces lean eye-of-round steak, cut into 1/2-inch chunks

1 large potato, peeled and cut into 1/2-inch pieces

1 onion, peeled and cut into 1/2-inch pieces

1 can whole tomatoes, chopped and drained

2 carrots, peeled and sliced in 1/2-inch pieces

6 cups beef stock

Preheat a saucepan and add the meat. Stir the meat so that it browns on all sides. Add the stock and deglaze the pan. Add the remaining ingredients and bring to a boil. Reduce the heat and let the soup simmer for 20 to 30 minutes, until the vegetables are tender.

Servings	Calories	Protein	Carbohydrates	Fat
4	635	70 g	17 g	29 g

Cream of Potato Soup

1 large Russet potato, cut into 1/4-inch pieces

1/4 cup leeks, finely chopped

3 cups chicken stock

1 tsp salt

olive-oil-flavored cooking spray

Coat the surface of a large saucepan with olive-oil-flavored cooking spray. Sauté the leeks with the salt for 3 to 4 minutes. Add the remaining ingredients. Bring to a boil and cook for 20 to 30 minutes, until the potato pieces are tender.

Remove the mixture from the heat and let cool for 10 to 15 minutes. Pour batches of the mixture into a blender and process each batch on high until smooth. Return the blended mixture to the pot and reheat.

Servings	Calories	Protein	Carbohydrates	Fat
1	110	3 g	24 g	0 g

Crab and Corn Chowder

4 cups chicken stock

1 small can creamed corn

4 oz real crab meat

1/4 cup green onion, finely chopped

1/2 tsp salt

freshly ground pepper to taste

Bring the chicken stock to a boil in a small saucepan and add the remaining ingredients. When the soup returns to a boil, it's ready to serve.

Servings	Calories	Protein	Carbohydrates	Fat
2	183	14 g	30 g	2 g

Egg Drop Soup

2 plus 1/4 cups chicken stock

1 egg white, beaten

1 tsp cornstarch

1/4 cup green onion, chopped

Bring the 2 cups of chicken stock to a rolling boil. Dissolve the cornstarch in 1/4 cup of cold chicken stock and stir into the boiling stock. Stirring constantly, add the egg white. As you stir, the egg white will dissipate into thin streams or "egg drops". Add the green onion and serve.

Servings	Calories	Protein	Carbohydrates	Fat
1	60	5 g	9 g	0 g

Wonton Soup

12 wontons (see recipe on page 124)
2 cups chicken stock
1/4 cup green onion, chopped

Bring the stock to a boil in a small saucepan and add the wontons. Cook the wontons for about 10 minutes, then add the green onion.

Servings	Calories	Protein	Carbohydrates	Fat
2	263	21 g	25 g	8 g

Pea Soup

4 cups chicken stock
1 box frozen peas
1 carrot, finely chopped
3/4 cup onion, finely chopped
4 oz turkey ham, diced
1 tsp salt
cooking spray

Coat a medium saucepan with cooking spray. Sauté the onion and carrots with the salt over medium heat for about 10 minutes, until soft. Add the chicken stock and bring to a boil. Add the frozen peas and cook until they are heated through.

Transfer the soup in batches to a blender and puree until smooth. Return the soup to the pot and bring it back to a boil. Add the turkey ham. Lower the heat and simmer for 15 minutes, stirring occasionally.

Servings	Calories	Protein	Carbohydrates	Fat
2	208	19 g	26 g	2 g

Vegetable Soup

3 cloves garlic, finely minced

1 medium onion, chopped

2 stalks celery, chopped

2 potatoes, peeled and cubed

2 carrots, chopped

1 can whole plum tomatoes, drained, seeded, and chopped

1/2 small cabbage, chopped

6 cups chicken stock

1/4 cup fresh basil, finely chopped

1/4 cup fresh parsley, finely chopped

2 tsp salt

1 tsp black pepper

cooking spray

Coat a large saucepan or stock pot with cooking spray. Sauté the garlic over medium heat until soft. Add the remaining ingredients and bring to a boil over high heat. Reduce the heat and simmer for about 30 minutes, until the vegetables are tender. Add the seasonings and serve.

Servings	Calories	Protein	Carbohydrates	Fat
2	300	11 g	62 g	1 g

0

Bean Soup

2 cups dried beans, any combination of or all one kind

1 carrot, finely chopped

1 onion, finely chopped

1 tsp salt

Rinse the dried beans well, removing any stones or beans that float. Place the beans in a large saucepan, cover by 2 inches with fresh, cold water, and soak overnight.

Rinse and drain the beans. Return them to the pot and cover by 2 inches with water. Add the onion and bring to a boil over high heat. Reduce the heat and simmer for about 40 minutes, until tender, adding hot water as necessary to keep the beans well covered. Add the remaining ingredients and simmer for about 15 minutes, until the carrots are tender.

Using a hand blender or potato masher, break up the beans slightly to thicken the soup. Add salt, season to taste, and serve.

Servings	Calories	Protein	Carbohydrates	Fat
8	393	26 g	70 g	2 g

Pumpkin Soup

2 cups fresh pumpkin or yellow squash, peeled and cut into cubes

1 small onion, chopped

6 cups chicken stock

1/8 tsp dried tarragon

1/2 tsp salt

freshly ground pepper to taste

Bring the chicken stock to a boil in a large saucepan and add the pumpkin and onion. Reduce the heat and simmer for about 30 minutes, until the pumpkin is tender. Transfer the soup in batches to a blender and puree until smooth. Return the soup to the pot and bring back to a boil. Add the remaining ingredients and simmer for another 10 minutes. Add the seasonings and serve.

Servings	Calories	Protein	Carbohydrates	Fat
2	80	3 g	18 g	0 g

Lentil Soup

2 cups dried lentils
1 carrot, finely chopped
1 onion, finely chopped
1 tsp salt

Place the lentils in a colander and rinse with cold water, removing any stones or lentils that float. Add the lentils and onion to a large saucepan and cover with water by 2 inches. Bring to a boil over high heat. Reduce the heat and simmer for about 40 minutes, until the lentils are tender, adding hot water as necessary to keep the lentils well covered. Add the remaining ingredients and simmer for about 15 minutes, until the carrots are tender.

Using a hand blender or potato masher, break up the lentils slightly to thicken the soup. Add salt, season to taste, and serve.

Servings	Calories	Protein	Carbohydrates	Fat
4	338	24 g	59 g	1 g

Marinated Salads

Cucumber Tomato Salad

1 cucumber, peeled, split lengthwise and sliced in 1/4-inch chunks

3 whole tomatoes, chopped

1 Tbs fresh basil, finely chopped

1 Tbs balsamic vinegar

salt and pepper

Combine all of the ingredients in a bowl. Mix well and season to taste with salt and pepper.

Servings	Calories	Protein	Carbohydrates	Fat
1	116	5 g	25 g	1 g

Cucumber Yogurt Salad

1 cucumber, peeled and thinly sliced

2 Tbs non-fat yogurt

1 clove garlic, finely minced

1/2 tsp salt

1 tsp fresh dill, finely chopped

Combine all of the ingredients in a bowl and mix well.

Servings	Calories	Protein	Carbohydrates	Fat
1	73	5 g	14 g	1 g

Marinated Bean and Corn Salad

1 6 oz can red beans

1 6 oz can corn or cooked kernels from 2 ears of fresh corn

2 Tbs lemon juice

1/4 cup fresh parsley, chopped

1 Tbs Dijon mustard

salt and pepper

In a large bowl, whisk together the lemon juice and mustard with salt and pepper to taste. Add the corn, beans, and parsley. Mix well, refrigerate for 2 hours, and serve.

Servings	Calories	Protein	Carbohydrates	Fat
2	171	7 g	34 g	2 g

Green Salads

I'm not going to spend a whole lot of time here stating the obvious advantages of green salads for adding volume to the bodybuilder's diet (see Chapter 9: Big Food For Big Appetites, page 169). However, for those of you who don't immediately understand, I offer the following:

Any leafy green vegetable——as well as watery veggies like tomatoes, peppers, cucumbers, celery, broccoli, cauliflower, and mushrooms——can be eaten in abundance. You don't need to pay much attention to calorie counts, because your body will expend more energy processing the fiber in these vegetables than it will obtain in calories. For example, a stalk of celery contains about 5 calories. Your body will expend the majority of those 5 calories processing the cellulose that, along with water, makes up bulk of the celery. The calories that remain are insignificant.

Do you get the picture? At the end of a grueling day that has left you with an appetite as voracious as a raging forest fire, you can eat a very large——bordering on obscene——salad (including your measly 6-ounce chicken breast), without adversely affecting your diet.

When you can't stand the hunger, a prodigious
helping of greens can make life much more
bearable and keep you from doing
something you may later regret.

Romano's Secret

This is my secret no-
calorie salad dressing that
you can use in abundance
to flavor your veggies.

1 Tbs Dijon mustard
1/3 cup balsamic vinegar
1 tsp garlic salt
2 packets Equal sweetener

Combine the ingredients in a small jar, cover tightly, and shake. Pour it on.
You can't beat that for simplicity.

Servings	*Calories*	*Protein*	*Carbohydrates*	*Fat*
8	*4*	*0 g*	*0 g*	*0 g*

Non-fat Italian Dressing

1 cup balsamic vinegar

1 clove garlic, finely minced

1 Tbs fresh basil, finely chopped

1/2 tsp salt

1/2 tsp pepper

1 tsp dry mustard or 2 Tbs prepared mustard

Mix all of the ingredients in a bowl with a wire whisk.

Servings	Calories	Protein	Carbohydrates	Fat
12	7	0 g	1 g	0 g

Non-fat Oriental Dressing

1 cup rice vinegar

2 Tbs low-sodium soy sauce

1 tsp toasted sesame seeds

Mix all of the ingredients in a bowl with a wire whisk. Tastes great on any combination of greens!

Servings	Calories	Protein	Carbohydrates	Fat
12	6	0 g	0 g	0 g

Non-fat Creamy Lemon Garlic Dressing

*1 cup non-fat yogurt cheese

1 clove garlic, finely minced

1/2 tsp salt

1 Tbs lemon juice

1 Tbs cilantro, finely chopped

1/2 tsp black pepper

Mix all of the ingredients in a bowl with a wire whisk.

Servings	Calories	Protein	Carbohydrates	Fat
12	10	1 g	2 g	0 g

*To make yogurt cheese, empty a container of plain non-fat yogurt into the center of a double-layer 10-inch square of cheesecloth. Bring the corners up to form a sack and tie with string. Hang the sack from the faucet of your kitchen sink for 4 hours, until all of the moisture has dripped out. The sack now contains yogurt cheese.

Chapter Three

VEGETABLES AND SIDE DISHES

A s a kid, I could always count on my mom, the best cook in the world, to fix some kind of greens almost every night. We enjoyed not only kale, but escarole, beet tops, Swiss chard, collard greens, turnip greens, broccoli rabbi, spinach, mustard greens, and endive, to name but a few. She prepared the vegetables in a variety of ways that never left us discontented——except of course for my sister who, if not for the invention of peanut butter, would have died as a child.

There are a number of reasons why healthy bodybuilders should include greens in their diet. By the way, the term "healthy bodybuilder" is not necessarily an oxymoron, like "honest lawyer" or "jumbo shrimp". Building a world-class body starts with world-class nutrition.

First, greens are especially important for the dieting bodybuilder. At less than 30 calories per cup, a proverbial mountain of greens can be had for a molehill of calories. Prepared as I demonstrate, greens can be just the ticket to squelch the racket of an angry, empty belly.

As the usual bodybuilder's diet progresses, it becomes more and more monotonous: chicken breast and rice, fish and rice, egg whites and oatmeal, on and on. Due to the relatively low fiber content of these foods, cobwebs may begin to grow in the bathroom. A prodigious helping of greens every day will ensure adequate pipe cleaning and regularity. (Each cup of greens contains about 1000 mg of fiber.)

Poor diet nutrition (and yes, chicken and rice to the exclusion of everything else is poor nutrition) combined with intense physical exercise can ravage the immune system. In his excellent book, Optimum Sports Nutrition, Dr. Michael Colgan cites numerous medical studies which show conclusively that athletes undergoing intense training develop immune deficiencies. In fact, viral infections proved more disabling than physical injuries. Vitamin C and beta-carotene, well-known immune boosters, are abundant in dark green leafy vegetables.

If only to add guiltless mass to your meals, eat greens every day. Greens can play a major role in your optimal nutrition program. Bodybuilders who want to grow up big and strong have to eat their spinach. However, don't let the obsessive nature of bodybuilding turn you into an uncontrolled grazer. Eating excessive amounts of fiber can cause the cobwebs to migrate from the bathroom to the rest of the house.

The following recipes contain just a few of the ways you can prepare your daily greens. The methods are interchangeable for most varieties, so be creative and enjoy one of God's greatest gifts to the diet.

Steamed Vegetables

Almost all green leafy vegetables can be steamed with aromatic herbs to create a healthy side dish. More tender varieties, like escarole and spinach, can be added to salads and eaten raw. Use your imagination——greens can greatly improve the quality of your diet.

Vegetables like broccoli, carrots, corn, squash, green beans, new potatoes, and mushrooms are delightful when steamed.

Place a steaming rack or metal sieve in the bottom of a large saucepan, and add just enough water to cover the legs of the rack. Once the water is boiling, arrange the vegetables on the rack. Pile them loosely on top of each other until the pot is nearly full. Cover and let the vegetables steam for 5 to 10 minutes, until tender.

Grilled Vegetables

Fleshy vegetables like zucchini, yellow squash, carrots, and eggplant taste best when grilled.

Split the vegetables in half lengthwise and coat the cut side with cooking spray. Grill cut-side down on a preheated grill over medium heat for 5 to 10 minutes, until tender. Serve grilled side up so that the grill marks can be seen.

Vegetables should be cooked as quickly as possible or eaten raw to preserve their color and nutritional value. Because of their subtle flavor, vegetables are easily overpowered by other ingredients. Cooking or serving them with sauces or in casseroles disguises their flavor and adds unneeded calories.

Kale Marinara

4 cups fresh kale, stems trimmed

3 cloves garlic, finely minced

1 cup crushed tomatoes

1 tsp salt

1/2 tsp pepper

1/4 cup fresh basil, chopped

olive-oil-flavored cooking spray

Rinse the kale in a colander to remove any grit. Coat a large saucepan with olive-oil flavored cooking spray and sauté the garlic until it just starts to turn brown. Add the tomatoes, salt, pepper, and basil. Reduce the heat and simmer, stirring occasionally, for about 10 minutes, until the sauce begins to thicken. Add the kale and stir to coat with the sauce. Cover and cook for about 10 minutes, until tender.

Servings	Calories	Protein	Carbohydrates	Fat
2	71	4 g	14 g	1 g

Spinach and Garlic

4 cups spinach, cleaned and trimmed

3 cloves garlic, very finely minced

1 tsp salt

olive-oil-flavored cooking spray

Rinse the spinach in a colander to remove any grit. Coat a large saucepan with olive-oil flavored cooking spray. Sauté the garlic over medium heat for about 2 minutes, until opaque. Add the drained, but still wet, spinach, and the salt. Stir and cover. Raise the heat to high and steam for about 5 minutes, until tender.

Servings	Calories	Protein	Carbohydrates	Fat
1	60	7 g	11 g	0 g

Beets with Tops

When you buy beets, look for medium-sized bulbs with big dark green tops. This recipe requires only beets and beet tops with just a little salt to taste.

Cut the tops from the beets and trim any tough looking stems. Soak the tops in a sink full of cold water to remove any grit. Drain in a colander. Peel the outer skin from the beets with a vegetable peeler. Cut the beets into quarters, wash, and drain. You may want to use gloves for this procedure——the Indians used to make dye from this stuff.

Add the beet quarters to a large saucepan and cover with 1 inch of water. Add about 1 teaspoon of salt and bring to a boil. Cook the beets for 10 minutes, until firm, then add the drained tops and cover. Continue to cook for about 5 minutes, until the tops are steamed.

Servings	Calories	Protein	Carbohydrates	Fat
1	52	2 g	11 g	0 g

Swiss Chard

4 cups Swiss chard, cleaned, washed, and drained

1 Tbs shallots, finely minced

1 tsp salt

1/2 tsp pepper

olive-oil-flavored cooking spray

Coat a large saucepan with olive-oil flavored cooking spray. Sauté the shallots over medium heat for about 2 minutes, until soft. Add the drained but still wet chard and the salt and pepper. Stir and cover. Raise the heat to high and steam for about 5 minutes, until tender.

Servings	Calories	Protein	Carbohydrates	Fat
1	31	3 g	7 g	0 g

Escarole with White Beans

4 cups escarole, trimmed, washed, and drained

1 cup cooked white beans

2 cups chicken stock

2 tsp salt

1/4 tsp crushed red pepper

Bring the chicken stock to a boil in a large saucepan. Add the escarole and the salt. Cover and cook for about 10 minutes, until tender. Add the beans and the red pepper, cover, and remove from the heat. Let stand for about 5 minutes, until the beans are warmed through.

Servings	Calories	Protein	Carbohydrates	Fat
2	138	9 g	26 g	1 g

Collard Greens

4 cups collard greens, trimmed, washed, drained

2 cloves garlic, finely minced

1/2 tsp crushed red pepper

1/2 cup chicken stock

1 chicken bullion cube

Dissolve the bullion cube in the chicken stock, then bring to a boil in a large saucepan. Add the garlic, red pepper, and cook for about 5 minutes. Add the collard greens, cover, and cook for about 15 minutes, until tender.

Servings	Calories	Protein	Carbohydrates	Fat
1	74	6 g	14 g	1 g

Eggplant Soufflé

1 large eggplant

1 onion, finely chopped

3 cloves garlic, finely minced

1/2 tsp salt

4 egg whites

olive-oil-flavored cooking spray

Preheat the oven to 350°F. Prick the eggplant in several places with a knife and place in a baking dish. Bake for about 1 hour, until wrinkled and soft. Let cool enough to be handled.

In the meantime, coat a saucepan with olive-oil-flavored cooking spray and add the onions, garlic, and salt. Sauté over low heat until the liquid is reduced and the onion and garlic mixture is very soft. Remove from the heat and set aside to cool.

Cut the eggplant open and scoop the insides into a bowl. Add the onion and garlic mixture and mix together with the eggplant. In a separate bowl, beat the egg whites until stiff peaks form when the beater is lifted. Add 1/4 of the beaten egg whites to the eggplant and stir to loosen the mixture. Using a rubber spatula, gently fold in the remaining egg whites.

Coat four 4-ounce ramekins with olive-oil-flavored cooking spray. Line the bottom of each with a disk of parchment paper and fill with the eggplant mixture. Bake at 350°F in a water bath (see page 25) for 30 to 40 minutes, until set. Let cool on a wire rack, then run a knife around the sides of the ramekin to loosen. Unmold and serve.

Servings	Calories	Protein	Carbohydrates	Fat
4	50	5 g	8 g	0 g

Orange Baked Yams

5 medium yams, peeled and cut into 1-inch chunks

1 plus 1/4 cup fresh-squeezed orange juice

1 tsp cinnamon

1/4 tsp cloves

2 Tbs brown sugar

1 Tbs cornstarch

Preheat the oven to 400°F. Arrange the yam chunks in a baking dish. Combine the cinnamon, cloves, brown sugar, and 1 cup of the orange juice in a bowl. Mix well with a wire whisk. Pour the mixture over the yams. Cover with aluminum foil and bake for about 40 minutes, until the yams are tender. Watch out for escaping steam when you uncover the pan!

Transfer the yam pieces into a serving bowl and pour the cooking liquid into a small saucepan. Bring the liquid to a boil and reduce by 2/3. Mix the cornstarch in the remaining 1/4 cup of orange juice. Remove the pan from the heat and stir in the cornstarch mixture. Continue to stir until the sauce thickens. Pour over the yams and serve.

Servings	Calories	Protein	Carbohydrates	Fat
4	241	3 g	57 g	1 g

Yam Casserole

5 medium yams, peeled and sliced in 1/4-inch rounds
4 tsp Butter Buds
1/2 cup maple syrup
1 tsp cinnamon
cooking spray

Preheat the oven to 350°F. Coat a baking dish with cooking spray and arrange a layer of yam slices on the bottom of the pan. Brush the slices liberally with maple syrup and sprinkle with Butter Buds and cinnamon. Repeat this process until the yam slices are used up.

Bake until the yams are golden and a fork can easily be inserted into their centers. Remove from the oven and let cool slightly before serving.

Servings	Calories	Protein	Carbohydrates	Fat
4	247	3 g	59 g	1 g

Mashed Potatoes

4 medium potatoes, peeled

1/2 cup non-fat milk

1 Tbs Butter Buds

1/2 tsp salt

1/4 tsp black pepper

Cut the potatoes into large chunks and boil in a large saucepan for about 20 minutes, until very tender. Drain in a colander and combine with the rest of the ingredients in a bowl. Beat with a wire whisk or electric mixer until light and fluffy.

Servings	Calories	Protein	Carbohydrates	Fat
4	234	6 g	53 g	0 g

Vege-Fuel-Fortified Mashed Potatoes

There are two ways to prepare Vege-Fuel-fortified mashed potatoes: my way and the easy way. The easy way is to buy a package of instant, fat-free mashed potatoes, measure out a serving of potato dust, and mix in the Vege Fuel. Prepare the mashed potatoes according to the package directions, and serve.

My way involves using real potatoes prepared as follows:

2 medium potatoes, peeled

1 cup non-fat milk

2 tsp Butter Buds

1 tsp salt

1/2 tsp freshly ground black pepper

1 scoop Vege Fuel™ *(100% pure isolated protein supplement from* TWINLAB®*)*

Cut the potatoes in to small cubes and boil in 1 quart of lightly salted water for about 15 minutes, until very soft. Drain in a colander and return to the pot.

Combine the Vege Fuel, milk, salt, pepper, and Butter Buds in a blender. Pulse the blender several times to break up any lumps. Add the mixture to the potatoes. Using a hand beater, whip the potatoes until light and fluffy. Adjust the seasonings and serve.

Servings	Calories	Protein	Carbohydrates	Fat
4	159	10 g	29 g	0 g

Chapter Four
CASSEROLES AND MEATLESS MEALS

V ege Fuel is a state-of-the-art soy protein supplement from TWINLAB. Although the source of the protein in Vege Fuel is soy, its protein quality has been tested against meat, fish, and egg, and has been found to meet or exceed the assayed levels of the individual amino acids for each of the aforementioned protein sources.

This is significant because unlike animal source proteins, Vege Fuel contains no cholesterol, no lactose, and scarcely a trace of fat. Vege Fuel has a high digestive efficiency, thus increasing the bioavailability of the protein.

One of the major benefits to using Vege Fuel for people trying to cut down on fat and cholesterol, is its lack of it. Vege Fuel is completely free of those nasty ingredients found in animal products yet is a complete source of protein. But, more remarkably, Vege Fuel can actually reduce your cholesterol level, help to prevent heart disease and help prevent certain types of cancer. Recent studies have also been conducted which show the potential roll of soy protein on positive kidney function and bone health.

In February 1994, the first international symposium on the Role of Soy in Preventing and Treating Chronic Disease convened in Mesa, Arizona. Over 45 researchers held technical sessions over a two and a half day period covering the topics of soy foods and their effect on heart disease and cancer. The symposium was prompted by a 1989 University of Alabama study showing that animals eating soybeans, added to a normal diet, developed significantly fewer breast cancers than animals on the same diet without soy. Additionally, studies on Japanese men and women, who's diets are rich in soy, showed they developed breast and prostate cancer at only a fraction of the rate as men and women in the U.S., where the consumption of soy is relatively low. Scientists also found that when the Japanese migrate to the U.S. or Europe, their rate of invasive breast and prostate cancer rises dramatically in only a few short years.

TWINLAB has long endorsed the use of soy in light of its apparent health benefits. In support of its product Vege Fuel, TWINLAB sent its head of customer service to monitor the symposium. The information she returned with is quite encouraging, It seems that soy contains at least one cancer-fighting isoflavone called *genestein*, which has shown to help reduce the risk of carcinogenesis in groups at risk for breast and prostate cancer.

There is overwhelming evidence that increased exposure to, and high levels of estrogens, increase the risk of breast cancer. Traditionally, Asian women—living in Asia, have lower endogenous estrogen levels than women living in the U.S.—both before and after menopause women. Human estrogen is widely used to relieve the effects of menopause, although many women are reluctant to take it because of the side effects and the possible cancer risks. A recent study at the University of

Manchester in England, suggests that soy estrogen acts on the same chemical targets in the body that human estrogen affects, although it is 1,000 times *less* potent. Doctors have also noticed a rarity of menopausal symptoms in women living in Asian countries where soy consumption is common. In fact, there is no phrase in Japanese for "hot flash."

Evidence further suggests that premenopausally they have lower progesterone levels.[1] These lower levels of endogenous hormones may be the result of a diet high in soy and are enough to explain the remarkably low breast cancer rates in Asian women. In fact, their menstrual cycle lasts on the average of five days longer than western women.

To evaluate this theory, a pilot study of the chemopreventive properties of soy protein in breast cancer is presently being conducted at the University of California at San Francisco. The test subjects are having, incorporated into their diets, two servings per day of Supro isolated soy protein, (the same soy protein isolate found in Vege Fuel). The subjects will be evaluated every three months and the results compared to a control group.[3] The anticipated favorable outcome of the study could put Vege Fuel at the forefront of the new wave of cancer and heart disease prevention supplements that have become the rage in the highly competitive health food arena.

There are many biologically plausible reasons why the consumption of soy could slow or prevent the onslaught of cancer. At most every stage of the cancer process, known naturally occurring chemicals found in food can alter the likelihood of carcinogenesis.[2] The isoflavones found in soy, specifically genestein, can act as antioxidants to effectively disable carcinogenic potential. Vege Fuel contains 20 mg. of isoflavone per 20 grams of protein, while animal protein contains none. The recommended dose for chemoprevention is 40 mg. per day.

Reducing total cholesterol, and raising high density lipoproteins (HDL), is a popular topic these days and was no less regarded at the symposium. Soy protein has been found to consistently elevate plasma thyroxine levels in different animals.

Plasma thyroxine change precedes plasma cholesterol change, the basis for the hypocholesterolimic effect of soy.[6] Although this effect is not completely understood, it is widely known that animal proteins can elevate cholesterol in test subjects, while test subjects fed diets of soy and other plant proteins had lower cholesterol levels.[7] The earliest clinical descriptions of a plasma cholesterol reduction after changing from animal to vegetable proteins, go back to the 1940s. These studies noted that in moderately elevated cholesterol patients, substitution of animal proteins with a textured soybean product, lowered cholesterol levels by more than 20%.[8]

Diet therapy is usually the first step in the treatment of hyperlipidimia. However, some patients are unable to lower their cholesterol to a desirable range with diet alone. For primary prevention of coronary disease, doctors and patients often wish to avoid pharmacological therapy of elevated cholesterol levels. The use of diet supplements such as soluble fibers, garlic, and soy protein may allow target lipid levels to be reached without the use of drugs.[4]

Recent research at the University of Illinois and elsewhere showed that soy protein isolates (Supro), and its isoflavones (Genestein), are dietary constituents that are effective in decreasing the risk of cardiovascular disease. If acceptable soy based foods can be developed, the use of these products in typical diets can be increased.[5]

If the foregoing is not enough for you to run out to your local GNC and pick up a container of Vege Fuel, perhaps this will: bodybuilders are typically at a higher risk for elevated cholesterol. This is due to the fact that bodybuilders eat a considerable amount of meat and other animal products to satisfy their supernormal protein requirements. Add to that fact the possibility of anabolic steroid use, a known cause of abnormal cholesterol levels, and perhaps a family history of heart disease, you just could have a hand grenade, minus it's pin, where your heart is supposed to be. Heart attacks are not uncommon among bodybuilders, I've seen a couple drop at Gold's in Venice over the years.

The health benefits of soy is overwhelmingly positive. Don't just look healthy, be healthy. Try Vege Fuel today and reap the benefits science has to offer.

REFERENCES

1. *Diet, Hormones, and Risk of Female Cancers.* MC Pike. Department of Preventative Medicine, School of Medicine, University of California, Los Angeles, CA.

2. *Diet, Phytochemicals, and Cancer Risk.* JD Potter. Division of Epidemiology, School of Publiuc Health, University of Minnesota, Minneapolis, MN.

3. *A Clinical Trial of the Chemopreventive Effect of a Soy Beverage in Women at High Risk for Breast Cancer.* N. Petrakis, J. Winkie, L. Coward, M. Kirk, and S. Barnes. Department of Epidemiology, University of california, San Francisco, CA and Department of Pharmacology, University of Alabama at Birmingham, AL.

4. *Perspectives on Soy Protein as a Non-Pharmacological Approach for Lowering Cholesterol.* AC Goldberg. Washington University School of Medicine, St. Louis, MO.

5. *Dietary Incorporation of Soy Products for Use in Clinical Studies.* BP Klein. Department of Foods and Nutrition, University of Illinois, Urbana, IL.

6. *Soy Protein, Thyroid Function, and Cholesterol Reduction.* W. Forsythe. Food and Nutrition Department, School of Home Economics, University of Southern Mississippi, South Station, Hattiesburg, MS>

7. *Soy Consumption and Cholesterol Reduction: Review of Animal and Human Studies.* KK Carroll, EM Kurowska. Center for Human Nutrition, Department of Biochemistry, University of Western Ontario, London, Ontario, Canada.

8. *Soy and Cholesterol Reduction: Clinical Experience.* CR Sirtori, E Grossi Paoletti. Center for Institute of Pharmacological Sciences, University of Milano, Milano, Italy.

Vege Fuel Main Courses

Vege Fuel can be added to just about any dish to improve its protein content. (Two scoops of Vege Fuel can also be added to any canned soup, stew, or sauce. Just remember to add the Vege Fuel to the food before heating, mix it in thoroughly, and heat the dish slowly.) The idea behind these Vege Fuel recipes is to significantly fortify food products containing little or no protein, creating an economical and practical replacement for a meat meal. Although Vege Fuel main courses contain protein levels comparable to meat, lack of fat and carbohydrates keeps calories to a minimum. On a restricted diet, this means more food over the course of the day and less racket from a belly aching to be fed.

For example: A can of Hain Naturals vegetarian black bean soup fortified with 2 scoops of Vege Fuel gives you a rather large bowl of a delicious and satisfying soup containing: 410 calories, 48 g carbohydrates, 54 g protein, and 1 g fat. An 8-ounce chicken breast and a 7-ounce yam delivers 532 calories, 50 g carbohydrates, 52 g protein, and 6 g fat. As you can see, the Vege-Fuel-fortified meal equals the traditional diet meal in protein and carbohydrates, yet saves 122 calories. On a 2000 calorie a day diet, the calories saved from the Vege Fuel meal can add up to one extra meal for an otherwise crabby individual. Do you see my point?

Spaghetti without Meatballs

4 oz pasta

1 cup tomato sauce (see recipe on page 89)

2 scoops Vege Fuel

Cook the pasta in 1 quart of lightly salted water until al dente. While the pasta is cooking, combine the Vege Fuel with the unheated sauce in a serving bowl and mix well. Drain the pasta completely and add to the sauce. Toss with 2 forks to coat the pasta. The hot pasta will heat the sauce. Serve immediately.

Servings	Calories	Protein	Carbohydrates	Fat
2	327	32 g	47 g	1 g

Tomato Sauce

2 cans chopped tomatoes with puree added
3 cloves garlic, finely minced
1/2 cup fresh basil, chopped
2 tsp salt
1 tsp freshly ground black pepper
olive-oil-flavored cooking spray

Coat a 2-quart saucepan with olive-oil-flavored cooking spray and sauté the garlic until it just starts to brown. Add the tomatoes, basil, salt, and pepper, and bring the sauce to a boil. Reduce the heat and simmer the sauce for about 10 minutes. Transfer the sauce to a large plastic container. (This sauce won't leave a nasty red stain on your Tupperware because it contains no fat.) Let cool, then refrigerate.

For extra protein, 2 scoops of Vege Fuel can be added to this sauce before heating.

Servings	Calories	Protein	Carbohydrates	Fat
8	48	2 g	12 g	0 g

Vege Fuel Lasagna

1 lb lasagna noodles

2 cups tomato sauce (see recipe on page 89)

4 scoops Vege Fuel

6 oz Alpine Lace non-fat mozzarella cheese

2 cups non-fat cottage cheese

3 Tbs grated parmesan cheese

2 egg whites

1/4 cup fresh parsley, chopped

1/2 tsp nutmeg

2 tsp salt

1 tsp freshly ground black pepper

1 Tbs cornstarch

Preheat the oven to 325°F. Boil the noodles in 1 quart of lightly salted boiling water for 5 to 7 minutes, just until they can bend easily. The noodles will be far from done, but don't worry; they will finish cooking in the oven. Drain the noodles and rinse them in cold water until they are cool enough to handle. Separate the noodles and hang them over the sides of the colander you used to drain them.

In a small bowl, combine the Vege Fuel with the tomato sauce and mix well. In another bowl, mix together 4 ounces of the non-fat mozzarella with the remaining ingredients until well blended.

Spread a small amount of sauce over the bottom of a 9- by 13-inch baking pan and layer in enough lasagna noodles (with their edges slightly overlapping) to cover the bottom of the pan. Evenly spread half of the cheese mixture over the surface of the noodles followed by a layer of sauce. Cover the sauce with another layer of noodles followed by the remaining cheese mixture, more sauce, then another layer of noodles. Top the final layer of noodles with the remaining sauce and the other 2 ounces of non-fat mozzarella sprinkled evenly over the surface.

Cover with aluminum foil and bake for 45 to 50 minutes, until golden brown on top. Let cool for 30 minutes before serving.

Servings	Calories	Protein	Carbohydrates	Fat
6	502	45 g	70 g	5 g

Macaroni and Cheese with Vege Fuel

4 oz elbow macaroni, uncooked

1 cup non-fat milk

2 slices Kraft Light cheddar cheese singles

2 scoops Vege Fuel

1 tsp salt

1/2 tsp freshly ground black pepper

2 Tbs flour

Preheat the oven to 350°F. Boil the macaroni in 1 quart of lightly salted water until tender. Meanwhile, mix the Vege Fuel with the milk in the blender. Pulse several times, until all of the lumps have dissipated. Pour the mixture into small saucepan and whisk in the flour. Bring the mixture to a boil over medium heat, whisking constantly, until the mixture begins to thicken.

Once the mixture starts to boil, reduce the heat to just barely boiling and continue to stir as the mixture begins to thicken. Continue to cook for 2 or 3 minutes, stirring constantly, until the mixture is smooth and free of lumps.

Break the cheese into small pieces and whisk them into the Vege Fuel mixture. Once the cheese is melted and blended, add the drained macaroni Remove from the heat and stir to evenly coat the pasta. Pour the macaroni and cheese into a baking dish and bake for 20 to 30 minutes, until golden brown on top.

Servings	Calories	Protein	Carbohydrates	Fat
2	403	39 g	55 g	2 g

Vege Fuel Yam Casserole

7 egg whites

1 whole egg

1 1/2 cups non-fat milk

4 scoops Vege Fuel

2 tsp cinnamon

1 tsp nutmeg

12 packets Sweet One sweetener

12 oz cooked yam, cut in 1/2-inch slices

Preheat the oven to at 375°F. Mix all of the ingredients except the yam in the blender. Pulse until smooth. Line a 9- by 13-inch baking pan with the yam slices, spacing them evenly. Pour the egg mixture over the yam slices. Cover the pan with foil and bake in a water bath (see page 25) for 1 hour, until firm. Let cool slightly before serving.

Servings	Calories	Protein	Carbohydrates	Fat
2	556	71 g	56 g	4 g

Spinach and Artichoke Pilaf

3 cups fresh spinach leaves, washed and chopped

1 cup canned artichoke hearts, drained, rinsed, and quartered

1/2 cup peeled whole tomatoes, chopped and drained

1 medium onion, chopped

1/3 cup white rice

1 cup chicken stock

2 scoops Vege Fuel

2 tsp salt

1 tsp freshly ground black pepper

1/2 tsp dried oregano

olive-oil-flavored cooking spray

Preheat the oven to 350°F. Coat a large oven-safe pan with olive-oil-flavored cooking spray. Add the onion and salt and sauté until the onion starts to brown. Add the rice and continue to cook, stirring constantly, for about 3 minutes, until the rice starts to become more opaque.

Using a blender, dissolve the Vege Fuel in the chicken stock and add to the rice and onion mixture. Bring the mixture to a boil and add the spinach. Stir the spinach into the liquid until it wilts. Add the tomatoes, oregano, artichoke hearts, and black pepper. Bring the mixture back to a boil, cover, and bake for 30 minutes, until all of the liquid has been absorbed and the rice is tender.

Servings	Calories	Protein	Carbohydrates	Fat
2	225	30 g	28 g	1 g

Baked Macaroni and Eggplant

4 oz fusilli (twist) pasta

1/2 cup whole peeled tomatoes

1 cup eggplant, cut into cubes

1/2 medium onion, chopped

1 cup non-fat milk

2 Tbs flour

2 scoops Vege Fuel

2 tsp salt

3 cloves garlic, finely minced

1/4 cup fresh basil, chopped

1/2 tsp freshly ground black pepper

2 Tbs grated Parmesan cheese

olive-oil-flavored cooking spray

Preheat the oven to 350°F. Coat a sauté pan with olive-oil-flavored cooking spray and sauté the garlic and onion with the salt. Once the liquid has evaporated and the onions begin to brown, add the eggplant and continue to cook for about 10 minutes, until the eggplant is tender but not mushy. Add the tomatoes, basil, and black pepper. Continue to cook for another 10 minutes.

Meanwhile, cook the pasta in 1 quart of lightly salted water until al dente. While the pasta cooks, mix the Vege Fuel and the milk in a blender. Pour the mixture into small saucepan and whisk in the flour. Bring the mixture to a boil over medium heat, whisking constantly, until the mixture begins to thicken. Continue to cook, whisking constantly, until the mixture is smooth. Remove from heat and whisk in the grated cheese.

Add the eggplant mixture to the Vege Fuel mixture and blend well. Add the pasta and toss to coat. Coat a 9- by 9-inch baking pan with olive-oil-flavored cooking spray and fill with the mixture. Bake for about 30 minutes, until golden brown.

Servings	Calories	Protein	Carbohydrates	Fat
2	475	43 g	64 g	5 g

Corn and Tomato Casserole

1 can peeled whole tomatoes, chopped and drained

2 cups canned corn

1/2 cup red bell pepper, chopped

1/2 cup onion, chopped

3 cloves garlic, finely minced

2 Tbs cilantro, finely chopped

2 tsp salt

1/2 tsp freshly ground black pepper

1 cup non-fat milk

2 scoops Vege Fuel

2 Tbs flour

cooking spray

Preheat the oven to 350°F. Coat a saucepan with cooking spray. Sauté the garlic, onion, bell pepper, and salt until the liquid has evaporated and the onion begins to brown. Add the corn and continue to sauté until the corn just starts to brown. Add the tomatoes, cilantro, and black pepper. Mix well and remove from the heat.

Using a blender, dissolve the Vege Fuel in the milk and pour the mixture into a small saucepan. Bring to a boil while whisking in the flour. As the mixture comes to a boil, reduce the heat and continue whisking until it thickens. Continue to cook, whisking constantly, until it is smooth.

Coat a baking dish with cooking spray. Mix the Vege Fuel mixture with the corn mixture in the dish until well blended. Bake for about 30 minutes, until golden brown.

Servings	Calories	Protein	Carbohydrates	Fat
2	470	37 g	78 g	2 g

Vege Fuel Quiche

You may have heard the saying: "Real men don't eat quiche." Indeed. I would bet that all of you "real men" would eat tree bark if you found out it had 93 grams of protein per serving. Wouldn't you rather have quiche?

Ham and Cheese Quiche

6 egg whites

1 cup non-fat milk

2 scoops Vege Fuel

4 oz turkey ham, cut into small cubes

1/2 tsp salt

1/2 tsp freshly ground black pepper

2 oz Alpine Lace non-fat cheese*

Preheat the oven to 325°F. Combine the egg whites, milk, Vege Fuel, salt, and pepper in a blender. Pulse several times, just enough to eliminate any lumps. Pour into an aluminum pie tin and set aside to rest, allowing the bubbles caused by blending to dissipate.

Meanwhile, brown the ham pieces in a non-stick pan. Pat the ham dry on paper towels to remove any fat, and add it to the egg mixture. Add the cheese and stir the mixture to evenly distribute the ingredients.

Cover the tin with aluminum foil and bake for about 1 hour, until a knife inserted into the center of the quiche can hold a small slit open. Allow the quiche to cool slightly and serve.

Servings	Calories	Protein	Carbohydrates	Fat
2	318	55 g	15 g	3 g

*Alpine Lace offers a variety of non-fat cheeses. Choose your favorite, or mix 2 or 3 different kinds. It's up to you. The nutritional content of each cheese is about the same.

Vegetable Quiche

6 egg whites

1 cup non-fat milk

2 scoops Vege Fuel

1 tsp salt

1/4 tsp freshly ground black pepper

1 cup sliced onion

1/2 cup green pepper, chopped

1/2 cup sliced mushrooms

cooking spray

Preheat the oven to 325°F. Combine the Vege Fuel, milk, and egg whites in a blender. Pulse several times, just enough to eliminate any lumps. Pour into an aluminum pie tin and set aside to rest, allowing the bubbles caused by blending to dissipate.

Meanwhile, coat a pan with cooking spray and add the onion and salt. Sauté over medium heat until the onions start to brown. Add the green peppers and mushrooms. Sauté until all of the water from the mushrooms has evaporated and the peppers are soft. Add the black pepper, remove from the heat, and allow to cool slightly.

Add the vegetables to the egg mixture and stir to evenly distribute the ingredients. Cover the tin with aluminum foil and bake until a knife inserted into the center of the quiche can hold a small slit open. Allow the quiche to cool slightly and serve.

Servings	Calories	Protein	Carbohydrates	Fat
1	457	80 g	32 g	1 g

Veggie Stew

1 large onion, chopped

1 leek, split and finely sliced

2 or 3 carrots, sliced

3 medium potatoes, peeled and diced

1 can peeled whole tomatoes, chopped and drained

8 oz fresh green beans, stemmed and cut in 1-inch pieces

2 zucchini, split and sliced

1/4 cup fresh basil, chopped

3 cloves garlic, finely minced

3 cups chicken stock

1 cup dry white wine

1 can corn, or the kernels from 2 ears

4 scoops Vege Fuel

3 tsp salt

2 tsp black pepper

cooking spray

Coat a large saucepan with cooking spray. Sauté the garlic, onion, and leek with the salt until they are soft and just starting to turn brown. Add the chicken stock and bring to a boil. Add the potatoes and carrots. Reduce the heat to a slow boil and cook the potatoes and carrots for about 10 minutes, until tender but still firm. Add the remaining vegetables, black pepper, and basil. Continue cooking for 5 to 7 minutes, until all of the vegetables are tender.

Ladle out 1 cup of liquid and combine it with the white wine in the blender. Add the Vege Fuel, pulsing until any lumps have disappeared. Slowly add to the stew, stirring constantly. Once it comes to a boil, it is ready to serve.

Servings	*Calories*	*Protein*	*Carbohydrates*	*Fat*
4	*302*	*31 g*	*46 g*	*1 g*

Chapter Five

PASTA, RICE, AND GRAINS

P asta, rice, and grains are the most versatile sources of complex carbohydrates. The recipes contained in this chapter just scratch the surface of what you can do with this food group. It's virtually impossible to eat as a bodybuilder and not consume large quantities of these foods. This chapter explains how to make these popular carbohydrates much more interesting.

Pasta

A while back I wrote an article called "Power Pasta", which included recipes based on pasta made from Jerusalem artichoke flour. Jerusalem artichoke pasta is much higher in protein than run-of-the-mill durum wheat pasta, making it a much smarter choice for bodybuilders.

Since then, I have developed a recipe for making pasta from scratch using Vege Fuel. Vege Fuel pasta is even higher in complete protein than Jerusalem artichoke pasta. You'll find the recipe in this chapter.

Although Vege Fuel pasta is the most nutritionally complete, you can use any kind of pasta in the Muscle Meals recipes, from plain supermarket durum wheat to health food store Jerusalem artichoke.

Entire books have been written on pasta, rice, and other grains with recipes from cultures stretching across the US, Europe, and the Orient. And why not? Grains are practically fat-free and come in a variety of shapes, flavors, and sizes. They are inexpensive, easy to cook, taste great, and can be prepared in many ways——you'll never get bored.

There's a simple rule to count the calories in carbohydrate foods. Roughly 1 ounce dry (give or take a few grams either way) equals 100 calories, about 20 g of carbohydrate, a few grams of incomplete protein, and very little fat.

Homemade pasta is not like microwave popcorn——it takes a lot of time and effort to prepare. It's messy and requires a great deal of kitchen space, not to mention hardware. If I haven't talked you out of it yet, you will find the finished product remarkable. Its protein content, flavor, and texture are superb. Ounce for ounce, Vege Fuel pasta contains 68 percent more protein, 25 percent fewer calories, and 50 percent less fat than regular durum wheat pasta.

Fresh pasta lasts almost indefinitely in the freezer, so you can consolidate your time in the kitchen by making a lot at once.

The pasta machines on the market today range from a fairly inexpensive hand-crank machine to an elaborate electrical device costing hundreds of dollars. With the electric model, you just dump the ingredients in one end and the finished product is extruded out the other. (My grandmother would roll over in her grave!) Whichever you choose, making pasta completely by hand is labor-intensive, but well worth it!

Basic Vege Fuel Pasta

6 egg whites

4 scoops Vege Fuel

3/4 cup flour

1 tsp salt

Mix the flour and Vege Fuel in a bowl. Make a well in the center of the mixture and add the egg whites. Gradually mix the ingredients until a stiff dough is formed. Don't worry if the dough is too sticky; the texture will change as you work with it. Mix 2 parts Vege Fuel to 1 part flour in a small bowl and use the mixture to dust your work surface and your hands as you handle the dough.

Turn the dough onto a dusted work surface and mold it into a ball. Knead the dough between the work surface and the heel of your hand several times, dusting the work surface with the Vege Fuel-flour mixture as necessary. Once the dough is firm and elastic, cover it and let it rest for 30 minutes.

Divide the dough into fourths and roll it out in your pasta machine. When the dough is rolled out to the thinness you desire, hang the strips on a portable clothes-drying rack. Allow the dough to air out for about 30 minutes, until it is no longer damp.

Cut the pasta into whatever shapes your machine will do and return the cut pasta to the drying rack to dry out completely. After the pasta dries, it can be cooked or frozen for future use.

This recipe makes two 4-ounce portions, and can be doubled as many times as you wish. I would, however, caution you against committing several dozen egg whites to the cause without first perfecting your technique on a smaller batch. After your first success you will find the process easy. It's time-consuming, but it's worth it!

Servings	Calories	Protein	Carbohydrates	Fat
2	398	62 g	36 g	0 g

To boost the protein content of a pasta meal even further, add Vege Fuel to the sauce.

Turkey and Onion Pasta

1 skinless, boneless turkey thigh, fat removed, cut into 1-inch cubes

8 onions, peeled, halved, and thinly sliced

cooking spray

1 and 1/2 cups chicken or turkey stock

2 Tbs grated Parmesan cheese

salt and pepper

8 oz pasta

Coat a saucepan with cooking spray and brown the turkey pieces. Stir in 2 teaspoons of salt and enough onions to fill the pot. Lower the heat to the lowest setting. Let the onions cook until very soft and almost all of the liquid has evaporated, stirring occasionally. If some of the onions don't fit into your pot, add them as those in the pot cook down.

Raise the heat to medium and add the stock 1/4 cup at a time. Stir until the stock is absorbed and reduced. The meat will have fallen apart, and the sauce will be very thick. Remove from the heat and stir in the grated cheese and black pepper until incorporated. Adjust the seasonings to taste.

Cook the pasta in 4 quarts of lightly salted boiling water until al dente. Drain, but reserve 1 cup of the cooking water. Return the drained pasta to the pot and add enough sauce to coat. Mix well, adding the reserved water if the mixture is too dry. Serve the pasta with extra sauce on top.

Servings	Calories	Protein	Carbohydrates	Fat
4	388	28 g	55 g	5 g

Pasta with Zucchini and Mushrooms

2 small zucchini, cut lengthwise into 1-inch pieces

1/2 basket fresh mushrooms, sliced

4 cloves garlic, finely minced

8 oz pasta

2 Tbs mint, chopped

2 Tbs balsamic vinegar

salt and pepper

olive-oil-flavored cooking spray

Coat a saucepan with olive-oil-flavored cooking spray. Sauté the garlic for about 2 minutes, until opaque. Add the vegetables and 1 teaspoon of salt. Lower the heat and sauté for about 5 minutes. Remove from the heat and let cool. Add the vinegar, mint, and pepper to taste and toss. Cover and refrigerate for at least 2 hours or overnight.

Let the zucchini and mushroom mixture sit until it reaches room temperature. Meanwhile, cook the pasta in 4 quarts of lightly salted boiling water until al dente. Drain and toss with the zucchini and mushroom mixture. Adjust the seasonings to taste and serve warm.

Servings	Calories	Protein	Carbohydrates	Fat
2	462	17 g	90 g	3 g

Pasta with Estive Sauce

8 oz whole plum tomatoes

2 tsp extra virgin olive oil

1/2 cup fresh basil, chopped

4 cloves garlic, crushed

1 tsp capers

salt and pepper

8 oz capellini pasta

Seed the tomatoes and chop. In a large bowl, combine the tomatoes with the basil, garlic, capers, oil, salt, and pepper. Cover and refrigerate overnight.

Remove the mixture from the refrigerator and let sit until it reaches room temperature.

Cook the pasta in 4 quarts of lightly salted water until al dente. Drain well. Remove the garlic pieces from the sauce and add the hot pasta. Toss and serve warm. This dish can be heated if desired.

Servings	Calories	Protein	Carbohydrates	Fat
2	506	17 g	95 g	7 g

Pasta with Red Pepper and Basil

2 red bell peppers, cut into 1/2-inch pieces

4 cloves garlic, minced

2 shallots, minced

1/2 cup white wine

1/4 cup fresh basil, chopped

8 oz pasta

1 Tbs grated Romano cheese

salt and pepper

olive-oil-flavored cooking spray

Blanch the peppers for about 2 minutes, until just tender. Immerse in ice water, drain, and set aside.

Coat a saucepan with olive-oil-flavored cooking spray. Sauté the garlic and shallots until opaque. Add the peppers and sauté for about 3 minutes, until the garlic and shallots begin to brown. Add the wine and reduce by about half. Remove from the heat.

Cook the pasta in 4 quarts of lightly salted boiling water until al dente. Drain, but reserve 1 cup of the cooking water. Return the peppers to the heat. Just as the liquid in the peppers starts to boil, add the pasta, basil, grated cheese, and black pepper. Toss, then remove from the heat. If the mixture is too dry, add enough of the reserved water to moisten. Adjust the seasonings to taste.

Servings	Calories	Protein	Carbohydrates	Fat
2	495	18 g	96 g	4 g

Pasta with Broccoli

1 1/2 cups broccoli florets

1 cup white wine

1/4 cup lemon juice

4 cloves garlic minced

2 shallots, minced

2 anchovies

black pepper

8 oz pasta

olive-oil-flavored cooking spray

Blanch the broccoli in lightly salted water for about 2 minutes. Immerse in ice water, drain and set aside.

Coat a saucepan with olive-oil-flavored cooking spray. Sauté the shallots and garlic until opaque. Add the white wine, lemon juice, and anchovies. Bring to a boil and dissolve the anchovies by mashing them against the bottom of the saucepan with the back of a wooden spoon. Reduce the liquid by half.

Cook the pasta in 4 quarts of lightly salted water until al dente. Drain and return to the pot. Add the broccoli and sauce. Toss, then let stand for 10 minutes. Toss again and serve.

Servings	Calories	Protein	Carbohydrates	Fat
2	525	21 g	101 g	4 g

Pasta and Veggies

1 small zucchini, cut into 3/4-inch slices

1 cup broccoli florets, blanched and cooled

1 small yellow squash, cut into 3/4-inch slices

1 cup mushrooms, sliced

6 cloves garlic, minced

3 shallots, minced

1 red bell pepper, cut into 3/4-inch pieces, blanched and cooled

2 Tbs fresh basil, chopped

2 Tbs grated Parmesan cheese

salt and pepper

olive-oil-flavored cooking spray

1/4 cup chicken stock

8 oz pasta

Steam the zucchini and yellow squash until tender. Coat a large saucepan with olive-oil-flavored cooking spray. Sauté the garlic and shallots until light brown. Add the mushrooms and sauté until wilted. Add the chicken stock and vegetables, tossing until lightly coated.

Cook the pasta in 4 quarts of lightly salted boiling water until al dente. Drain and return to the pot. Add the vegetables, basil, cheese, salt, and pepper. Toss and serve.

Servings	Calories	Protein	Carbohydrates	Fat
2	568	25 g	104 g	6 g

Pasta with Escarole and Beans

1 head escarole

16-ounce can of white beans, drained and rinsed

4 oz macaroni

4 cloves garlic, minced

salt and pepper

olive-oil-flavored cooking spray

Cook the macaroni in 2 quarts of lightly salted water until al dente. Drain and set aside.

Cut away the stump of the escarole and slice the head crosswise into 3 equal pieces. Separate the leaves and soak them in a sink full of cold water, then drain in a colander.

Coat a large saucepan with olive-oil-flavored cooking spray. Sauté the garlic until opaque. Add the still wet escarole and 1 teaspoon of salt and toss. Cover and cook for 10 minutes, stirring occasionally, until the escarole is completely wilted and tender.

Add the drained beans and pasta and cook for 2 minutes. Add salt and pepper to taste.

Servings	Calories	Protein	Carbohydrates	Fat
2	529	28 g	101 g	3 g

Green Beans and Pasta

8 oz young green beans

8 oz macaroni

1 can whole tomatoes, seeded, chopped, and drained

6 cloves garlic, minced

salt and pepper

olive-oil-flavored cooking spray

Coat a heavy saucepan with olive-oil-flavored cooking spray. Sauté the garlic until opaque. Add the tomatoes, salt, and pepper. Stir and cook for about 10 minutes. Wash and trim the beans, then cut into pasta-length slices. Add to the sauce, cover, and reduce the heat. Cook for about 5 minutes, until the beans are just tender. Remove from the heat.

Cook the pasta in 4 quarts of lightly salted boiling water until just al dente. Drain and add to the sauce. Toss and serve.

Servings	Calories	Protein	Carbohydrates	Fat
2	550	20 g	115 g	2 g

Tomato Sauce

1 can tomato puree

2 cans peeled whole tomatoes, chopped and drained

4 to 6 cloves garlic, minced

1/4 cup fresh basil leaves, chopped

salt and pepper

Combine the ingredients in a large saucepan. Bring to a boil, reduce the heat, and simmer for 1/2 hour.

Servings	Calories	Protein	Carbohydrates	Fat
1/2 cup	40	4 g	7 g	0 g

Marinara Sauce

3 cans whole, peeled tomatoes
6 cloves garlic, finely minced
1/4 cup fresh basil, chopped
1/4 cup fresh parsley, chopped
salt and pepper
olive-oil-flavored cooking spray

Squeeze the seeds and juice from the tomatoes and then drain in a colander. Coat a large saucepan with olive-oil-flavored cooking spray. Sauté the garlic until opaque. Add the tomatoes and mix well. Reduce the heat and add the herbs. Season with salt and pepper to taste. Cook for about 10 minutes over medium heat, stirring frequently. Remove from the heat, cover, and let stand for 2 hours or overnight.

Servings	Calories	Protein	Carbohydrates	Fat
16	35	1 g	8 g	0 g

Baked Pasta

3 oz pasta spirals
1 cup non-fat ricotta cheese
1/2 cup chopped canned tomatoes or tomato sauce
6 oz ground turkey breast
1 tsp garlic salt
1/2 cup non-fat mozzarella, shredded
olive-oil-flavored cooking spray

Preheat the oven to 375°F. Brown the turkey meat in a non-stick pan. Add the tomatoes and garlic salt. Simmer over low heat for about 10 minutes, until the tomatoes are soft. Meanwhile, cook the pasta in lightly salted water for about 8 minutes, until al dente. Once the sauce is cooked, add the ricotta and mix well. When this mixture boils again, add the drained pasta and toss to mix. Transfer the mixture to an oven-safe bowl or casserole and top with the mozzarella shreds. Coat the top lightly with olive-oil-flavored cooking spray and bake for 15 minutes, until the cheese is melted.

Servings	Calories	Protein	Carbohydrates	Fat
2	487	42 g	51 g	13 g

Rice

Rice, one of man's oldest foods, was first cultivated in Asia around 3000 BC. It has since evolved into a staple of the Asian diet, with some 300 pounds consumed per person each year. In this country, it's been relegated to a side dish; the average American consumes only 22 pounds per year. For bodybuilders, both rice and pasta are the major carbohydrate sources. Pasta may be more popular, but rice, for a number of reasons, is better.

First of all, rice contains more complex carbohydrates than pasta. A 1/2 cup serving of pasta contains 20 g of complex carbohydrates, while the same measure of rice contains 23 g. Rice is far more

versatile than pasta—it can even be eaten for dessert. It costs just 4 cents per 1/2 cup serving, and it's more easily digested since, unlike pasta, rice is free of gluten (the wheat protein that many people have difficulty digesting).

Rice's one drawback is its more complicated preparation. I have received letters that wax grim of cookware forever cemented with burned-on rice goop. Don't worry: if you can boil water, you can cook rice. In fact, rice does a lot of its cooking without any help. A rice steamer is by far the easiest way to cook rice. Just dump 1 part rice to 2 parts water into the cooker and turn it on. A short time later, you have perfect rice! If you don't own a rice steamer, the same proportion of rice and water goes into a pot. Bring it to a boil, and then lower the heat to a simmer. When the water level reaches the top of the rice, cover the pot, and remove it from the heat. The rice will finish itself in 20 minutes, and it won't burn. If you dare to get a little more elaborate, the following recipes are some of my favorites.

Fried Rice

2 cups cooked white rice (left over from the previous day)

2 egg whites

1/4 cup frozen peas

1 cup left over chicken breast pieces

1/2 cup bean sprouts

1 Tbs low-sodium soy sauce

1/4 cup drained bamboo shoots

cooking spray

Coat a sauté pan with cooking spray. Scramble the egg whites until very firm, then set aside.

Coat the pan with cooking spray again and sauté the bean sprouts, bamboo shoots, and peas until heated through. Remove and add to the reserved egg whites.

Re-spray the pan.

Cook the rice in the sauté pan, stirring occasionally, until it starts to brown. Add the chicken, soy sauce, bean sprouts, bamboo shoots, egg whites, and peas. Mix well.

Servings	Calories	Protein	Carbohydrates	Fat
2	415	39 g	46 g	8 g

Mixed Rice Pilaf

1/4 cup wild rice

1/2 cup long grain rice

1/2 cup brown rice

1/2 cup basmati or Tex-mati rice

3 cups chicken stock

1 tsp salt

1/4 cup green onion, chopped

Cook the wild rice in 1 quart of lightly salted boiling water for about 40 minutes, until tender. Drain and set aside.

Bring the chicken stock to a boil and add the remaining rice and salt. Return to a boil, cover, and reduce the heat to low. Let the rice cook for about 20 minutes, until most of the stock is absorbed. Add the wild rice and green onion. Remove from the heat and mix well. Cover and let stand for another 20 minutes, until all of the liquid is absorbed. Fluff the rice with a fork and serve.

Servings	Calories	Protein	Carbohydrates	Fat
2	214	4 g	48 g	0 g

Dirty Rice

8 oz Italian turkey sausages in casings

1 large onion, chopped

8 oz skinless, boneless chicken thigh meat

1 cup mushrooms

2 Tbs parsley, finely chopped

2 tsp gumbo file

1 chili pepper, chopped

1 cup white rice

2 cups chicken stock

salt and pepper

1/2 cup white wine

Preheat the oven to 350°F. Place the sausage in a sauté pan and pierce the skin in several places. Add water to halfway up the sides of the sausages. Cook over high heat, turning the sausages occasionally. After the water has boiled off, brown the sausage on all sides. Remove the sausage from the pan and drain on paper towels.

Brown the chicken in an oven-safe pan, then set aside with the sausages. Do not clean the pan. Add the onions, peppers, mushrooms, gumbo file, salt, and pepper. Cook over medium heat, stirring occasionally until all of the liquid evaporates and the onions start to brown. Add the rice and stir to coat. Add the chicken stock, wine, parsley, sausage, and chicken. Stir and cover. Bake for 30 to 40 minutes, until all of the liquid is absorbed.

Servings	Calories	Protein	Carbohydrates	Fat
2	369	31 g	37 g	10 g

Vege Fuel Rice

1/3 cup white rice, uncooked

1 cup chicken stock

1 tsp salt

2 scoops Vege Fuel

Preheat the oven to 350°F. Using a blender, dissolve the Vege Fuel in the chicken stock. Fill an oven-safe saucepan with the rice, then pour the Vege Fuel mixture over it.

Slowly bring the mixture to a boil, cover, and place in the oven. Bake for 30 minutes, until all of the liquid has been absorbed and the rice is tender.

Servings	Calories	Protein	Carbohydrates	Fat
1	285	50 g	21 g	0 g

Vege Fuel rice makes a nicely textured vehicle for a variety of flavors. Virtually any cooked vegetable or fresh herb can be added during the final stages of cooking.

After the rice has been in the oven for 10 minutes, stir in 1/2 cup to 1 cup of any cooked vegetable or 1 to 2 teaspoons of any fresh or dried herb. Mix well, cover, and continue to cook for another 15 to 20 minutes, until all of the liquid has been absorbed and the rice is tender.

The calories of additional herbs or vegetables would hardly be worth noting. Vege-Fuel-fortified tomato sauce (see recipe on page 67) can also be added to really boost the protein content while keeping the calories down.

Arroz con Pollo

1 lb chicken breasts, boned and skinned

2 cups tomatoes, chopped, drained, and peeled

1 Tbs cilantro, chopped

1 green chili, chopped

1 onion, chopped

1 cup white rice

2 cups chicken stock

salt and pepper

3 cloves garlic, minced

2 Tbs lemon juice

cooking spray

Cut the chicken into thin strips. Coat a large saucepan with cooking spray. Sauté the garlic until opaque. Add the chicken and sauté until it starts to brown. Remove the chicken and set aside on a covered plate. Do not clean the saucepan. Add the onion, peppers, salt, and pepper. Sauté until the onion starts to brown. Add the rice and stir to coat. Add the chicken stock, tomatoes, lemon juice, and cilantro. Bring to a boil, cover, and reduce the heat to low. Simmer for 20 minutes, until the remaining liquid is absorbed. Stir and remove from the heat. Cover and let stand for another 20 minutes. Fluff the rice and serve.

Servings	Calories	Protein	Carbohydrates	Fat
2	538	67 g	43 g	10 g

Paella

8 large shrimp, cleaned and deveined

1 lb chicken breasts, skinless, boneless, cut in 2-inch pieces

18 to 20 small clams or mussels

8 oz squid, cleaned and sliced into ringlets

1 can peeled whole tomatoes, chopped and drained

2 cups chicken stock

1/2 cup white wine

1 1/2 cups long grain white rice

2 Tbs parsley, chopped

1 cup canned artichoke hearts, drained and quartered

1/2 cup frozen peas, thawed

cooking spray

1/4 tsp saffron threads

1 large onion, chopped

1 large green pepper, chopped

4 cloves garlic, minced

salt and pepper

Preheat the oven to 375°F. Crush the saffron with a mortar and pestle and add it to the wine. Coat a large oven-safe saucepan with cooking spray. Add the chicken pieces in batches and brown them, reserving them in a covered dish. Do not clean the pan. Add the garlic, onions, peppers, salt, and pepper. Sauté over medium heat until the onions begin to brown. Add the rice and stir to coat. Add the tomatoes, stock, and wine. Bring to a boil, cover, and bake for 20 to 30 minutes, until the rice is al dente and very wet. Add the squid and shellfish, cover, and return to the oven. Cook for another 10 to 15 minutes or until the clams and mussels open. Discard any that do not open. Add the parsley, peas, and artichoke hearts and stir. Cover and let stand for 15 minutes.

Servings	Calories	Protein	Carbohydrates	Fat
4	543	75 g	40 g	8 g

G r a i n s   •

Grains are the basis for all starchy carbohydrates, including pasta and rice, and have the same nutritional benefits. Unlike pasta and white rice, however, unprocessed grains have the added fiber, vitamins, and minerals of the outer hull. Whole grains are also digested more slowly, providing sustained energy.

The most common grain food, after wheat flour products and rice, is oatmeal. This is unfortunate because there are a wide variety of healthy grains with much better taste and texture. Although you may not be familiar with them, give them a try. These recipes make it as easy as possible.

Wheat Berry Breakfast Pudding

zest from 1 lemon, finely minced

*1 cup cooked wheat berries

16 oz non-fat cottage cheese, pureed in a food processor

2 tsp vanilla

1 packets of unflavored gelatin

10 packets of Equal

1/2 tsp nutmeg

1/2 cup non-fat milk

1 tsp cinnamon

Dissolve the gelatin in 1/2 cup milk. Let stand for 2 minutes, then microwave on high for 40 seconds. Stir the gelatin and milk mixture into the cottage cheese and mix well. Add the remaining ingredients and mix well. Spoon into four 4-ounce bowls and chill for 4 hours or overnight, until set.

**3/4 cup of dry wheat berries cooked in 1 quart of lightly salted water will yield roughly 1 cup when drained.

Servings	Calories	Protein	Carbohydrates	Fat
2	401	63 g	29 g	3 g

Corn Parmesan Timbale

1 Tbs fresh parsley, chopped

1/2 cup cornmeal

2 cups chicken stock

1/2 tsp salt

1/2 cup white raisins

1/4 tsp black pepper

2 Tbs plus 2 tsp grated Parmesan cheese

cooking spray

Bring the stock to a boil in a medium saucepan and add the salt. While stirring the stock with a wire whisk, add the cornmeal in a slow, steady stream. Be sure to whisk away any lumps. Once all of the cornmeal is added, reduce the heat to low and add the raisins. Cook, stirring occasionally, for 5 to 7 minutes, until very thick. Remove from the heat and stir in the 2 tablespoons cheese, black pepper, and parsley. Coat four 4-ounce ramekins with cooking spray and fill. Level the top with a metal spatula. Let cool until firm.

Before serving, unmold the ramekins and place them top side down on a sheet pan that has been coated with cooking spray. Sprinkle with the remaining grated cheese and broil 2 inches from the flame until golden.

Servings	Calories	Protein	Carbohydrates	Fat
2	352	13 g	64 g	6 g

Tabbouli

1 packet tabbouli

1 1/2 cups fresh parsley, chopped

2 cloves garlic, minced

2 Tbs lemon juice

3 or 4 medium tomatoes, chopped

salt and pepper

2 Tbs fresh mint leaves, chopped

Cook the tabbouli according to the package directions, but do not add oil. In a small bowl, whisk the lemon juice, garlic, salt, pepper, and mint. Add the parsley, tomatoes, and this mixture to the tabbouli. Mix well.

Servings	Calories	Protein	Carbohydrates	Fat
1	320	11 g	61 g	3 g

Fragrant Barley

1 cup pearl barley

2 cups beef stock

cooking spray

2 carrots cut into 1/4-inch cubes

1 medium onion, chopped

1/2 tsp cinnamon

1/2 tsp salt

1/2 tsp black pepper

1 Tbs fresh mint, chopped

Coat a large saucepan with cooking spray. Add the onion, carrots, and salt. Sauté until the onion starts to brown. Stir in the cinnamon and black pepper. Add the barley and stir to coat. Add the beef stock and bring to a boil. Cover and simmer on low heat for 20 minutes. Stir and add the mint. Cover and let stand for another 20 minutes.

Servings	Calories	Protein	Carbohydrates	Fat
2	410	13 g	80 g	2 g

Growth Meal

1/4 cup whole oats

1/4 cup wheat berries

1/4 cup brown rice

1/2 cup rolled oats

1 cup non-fat milk

1 tsp cinnamon

1 tsp vanilla

6 to 8 packets of Equal sweetener

1/2 tsp salt

Bring 2 quarts of lightly salted water to a boil. Add the whole oats, wheat berries, and brown rice. Cook for 20 to 30 minutes, until the grains are tender. Drain and rinse. Heat the milk in a non-stick saucepan just until it boils. Lower the heat and add the cooked grains and rolled oats. Cook over medium heat for 3 to 5 minutes, until the mixture is thickened. Remove from the heat. Stir in the vanilla, cinnamon, and Equal. Adjust to taste.

Microwave Instructions:

In a microwave-safe bowl, add the milk, rolled oats, and cooked grains. Cook on high for 4 to 6 minutes. Stir in the vanilla, cinnamon, and Equal.

Servings	Calories	Protein	Carbohydrates	Fat
1	354	16 g	65 g	2 g

Vege Fuel Baked Cornmeal

3 oz coarse cornmeal

2 cups chicken stock

2 scoops Vege Fuel

1/2 cup peeled whole tomatoes

2 cloves garlic, finely minced

2 Tbs fresh basil, chopped

1/2 cup onion, finely chopped

1/2 tsp nutmeg

2 tsp salt

1/2 tsp freshly ground black pepper

cooking spray

Preheat the oven to 350°F. Mix the cornmeal, 1/2 teaspoon of salt, and Vege Fuel in a small bowl. Bring the chicken stock to a rolling boil and slowly drizzle in the cornmeal mixture while stirring constantly with a wire whisk. Continue to cook the cornmeal for about 5 minutes, until it thickens. Immediately pour the cooked cornmeal into a baking dish that has been coated with cooking spray. Spread it evenly across the bottom.

Coat a sauté pan with cooking spray. Sauté the garlic with the onion and the remaining salt until the liquid has evaporated and the onion begins to brown. Add the remaining ingredients and let the sauce simmer over medium heat for about 10 minutes, until thickened.

Pour the sauce over the corn mixture and bake for 30 minutes. Remove and let cool before serving.

Servings	Calories	Protein	Carbohydrates	Fat
1	601	54 g	95 g	1 g

Fried Vege Fuel Cornmeal

3 oz coarse cornmeal

2 cups chicken stock

2 scoops Vege Fuel

1 tsp salt

cooking spray

Mix the dry ingredients together in a bowl. Coat a 9- by 9-inch baking pan with cooking spray. Bring the chicken stock to a rolling boil and slowly drizzle in the cornmeal mixture while stirring constantly with a wire whisk. Lower the heat and continue to stir. Continue cooking until the mixture has thickened. Pour immediately into the coated baking pan.

As the cornmeal cools, it will solidify. Cut the solidified cornmeal into 4 pieces. Coat a pan with cooking spray and fry each piece on both sides over very low heat until brown.

The fried cornmeal can be served with honey or syrup for breakfast or topped with tomato sauce or sautéed vegetables for a main course.

Servings	Calories	Protein	Carbohydrates	Fat
1	524	51 g	78 g	1 g

Vege Fuel Oatmeal

2/3 cup oatmeal

1 1/4 cups cold water

2 scoops Vege Fuel

1 Tbs vanilla

1 tsp cinnamon

4 packets Equal sweetener

1/4 tsp salt

Pour the water into a saucepan and add the Vege Fuel. Mix well with a wire whisk until all lumps are gone. Add the oatmeal and bring to a boil, stirring constantly. Once the mixture starts to thicken, cover the pot and turn off the heat. Let the oatmeal steep undisturbed for 10 minutes.

Add the remaining ingredients and mix well.

Servings	Calories	Protein	Carbohydrates	Fat
1	456	60 g	37 g	5 g

Grits

3 oz yellow or white cornmeal

2 cups water

2 scoops Vege Fuel

5 packets Equal sweetener

1 tsp cinnamon

2 tsp vanilla extract

1/2 tsp salt

Mix the Vege Fuel with the salt and cornmeal in a bowl and blend well. Bring the water to a rolling boil and slowly drizzle in the cornmeal mixture while stirring constantly with a wire whisk. As the mixture thickens, lower the heat and continue to cook until the grits are very thick and bubbles leave craters on the surface. Remove from the heat, cover, and let stand for 10 minutes.

Add the remaining ingredients and mix well.

Servings	Calories	Protein	Carbohydrates	Fat
1	526	51 g	75 g	1 g

C h a p t e r   S i x

POULTRY

A fter fish, chicken and turkey are the leanest, lowest-calorie protein sources available. Six ounces of white meat, with skin and fat removed, have about 200 calories, 40 g protein, 0 g carbohydrates, and 3 g fat——which has made poultry a staple of most bodybuilders' diets. Because it is so low in fat, white meat can be very dry and unappetizing, especially if overcooked. Unfortunately, if you undercook poultry, you run the risk of becoming quite ill. According to a United States Department of Agriculture study, more than half of the chickens sold in US supermarkets contain salmonella bacteria. Because high heat kills salmonella, most people overcook chicken and deal with the dryness rather than risk potential illness.

The USDA has approved the use of trisodium phosphate (TSP) in poultry processing. TSP is an inexpensive chemical, widely known as a mild household cleanser. Testing has shown that dipping freshly killed and dressed birds into a solution of TSP is very effective at killing bacteria. TSP use does not have to be disclosed to the consumer, but even if you know that your poultry has been treated, you should still exercise caution in the kitchen. Even the USDA says that TSP isn't 100 percent effective against all contaminants.

Always keep poultry refrigerated or frozen until you are ready to cook it, and wash everything that comes in contact with the raw meat——including your hands. I can't stress enough the importance of keeping everything the raw poultry touches thoroughly washed. Spend just one day doubled up in pain on the couch in between trips to the bathroom to wrench your guts out and you too will share my concern.

Still, overcooking is not necessary. Cook poultry just until it is no longer pink inside and the juices run clear, or until it has an internal temperature of 160°F to 170°F. If you keep these fail-safe standards in mind, the following recipes might become your favorites.

Italian Chicken Salad

8 skinless, boneless chicken breasts, poached and cut into cubes

10 whole plum tomatoes, coarsely chopped

1/4 cup fresh basil, finely chopped

olive-oil-flavored cooking spray

4 cloves garlic, finely minced

2 shallots, finely minced

1 cup fresh oyster mushrooms, coarsely chopped

1 lb pasta

1/2 tsp salt

1/4 tsp ground black pepper

Combine the chicken, tomatoes, and basil in a bowl and mix well. Coat a sauté pan with olive-oil-flavored cooking spray. Sauté the garlic and shallots until soft. Add the mushrooms, salt, and pepper. Cook until most of the liquid from the mushrooms evaporates. Cool, and add to the chicken mixture.

Cook the pasta in 8 quarts of lightly salted water until al dente. Drain, cool under cold running water, and add to the chicken mixture. Toss, cover, and let stand in the refrigerator for 1 hour. Adjust the seasonings to taste before serving.

Servings	Calories	Protein	Carbohydrates	Fat
8	422	40 g	50 g	6 g

Chicken Piccata

4 skinless, boneless chicken breasts
juice of 2 lemons
1 Tbs capers
1/2 cup white wine
salt and pepper
olive-oil-flavored cooking spray

Pound the chicken breasts flat with a mallet or the side of a can. Sprinkle both sides of the chicken with salt and pepper. Coat a large saucepan with olive-oil-flavored cooking spray. Add the chicken and brown on both sides, but do not overcook. Place on a plate and cover. Add the white wine to the hot pan and scrape the bottom with a wooden spoon. Reduce the liquid by half. Return the chicken to the pan, and turn it over in the pan to coat. Add the capers and lemon juice, and bring to a boil. Remove the chicken, place on a serving plate, and cover with sauce.

Servings	Calories	Protein	Carbohydrates	Fat
2	362	62 g	3 g	9 g

Lemon Chili Chicken

4 chicken breasts, skinned and boned (save the bones)

6 lemons, juiced

6 cloves garlic, chopped

1/4 cup sliced chilies with juice

1 tsp salt

10 peppercorns

1 Tbs cilantro, finely chopped

1 bay leaf

1 1/2 cups chicken stock

1 Tbs arrowroot or cornstarch

Combine the chicken, lemon juice, garlic, chilies, salt, peppercorns, and cilantro in a bowl. Cover and refrigerate for 1 hour. Remove the chicken and set aside. Preheat the oven to 475°F. Place the bones in roasting pan and cover with the marinade. Roast the bones until very brown.

To make the sauce, pour the contents of the roasting pan into a saucepan. Add the chicken stock and bay leaf and reduce the liquid by half. Strain the liquid through a cheesecloth-lined strainer. Let stand undisturbed until the fat rises to the surface. Remove and discard the fat. Return the mixture to saucepan and reduce by half again. Dissolve the arrowroot or cornstarch in 1/4 cup of water and add the mixture to the sauce. Remove the sauce from the heat and stir until thick. Broil the chicken and serve with the sauce.

Servings	Calories	Protein	Carbohydrates	Fat
2	419	63 g	19 g	10 g

Chicken Stroganoff

2 skinless, boneless chicken breasts, cut into 3/4-inch pieces

1 cup sliced mushrooms

1 cup chicken stock

1/4 cup non-fat milk

1 Tbs cornstarch

4 shallots, sliced

2 tsp fresh parsley, chopped

8 oz fettucine

salt and pepper

1/2 tsp freshly ground nutmeg

cooking spray

Coat a saucepan with cooking spray. Brown the chicken and set aside. Respray the pan and sauté the shallots until opaque. Add the mushrooms and 1 teaspoon of salt. Cook over medium heat until mushrooms just begin to brown. Add the chicken and chicken stock. Reduce the liquid by half.

Dissolve the cornstarch in the milk and add to the sauce. Remove from the heat and stir until thickened. Add the parsley and nutmeg, and salt and pepper to taste.

Cook the pasta in 4 quarts of lightly salted boiling water until al dente. Drain and add to the sauce. Toss and serve.

Servings	Calories	Protein	Carbohydrates	Fat
4	330	24 g	49 g	4 g

Chicken Cacciatore

6 chicken breasts, skin and fat removed

cooking spray

1 small can tomato paste

1 can tomato puree

4 cloves garlic, minced

1/4 cup basil leaves, chopped

salt and pepper

Coat a pan with cooking spray and add 3 chicken breasts (bones up). Sprinkle with salt and pepper and half of the garlic. Cook over medium-high heat until brown, then turn and brown on other side. Set the chicken aside and cover. Repeat the process with the remaining chicken.

Add the tomato puree to the empty pot and stir with a wooden spoon, scraping up anything that is stuck to the bottom. Stir in the tomato paste and basil. Return the chicken to the pot and cover with sauce. Lower the heat and simmer for 30 to 40 minutes, until the chicken has loosened from the bones and the sauce is thick and adheres to the meat. This dish can be served with pasta or rice, or eaten by itself.

Servings	Calories	Protein	Carbohydrates	Fat
4	306	48 g	10 g	7 g

Chicken Hash

6 chicken thighs, boneless, with fat removed

2 medium potatoes, peeled and cut into 1/4-inch cubes

1 large onion, cut into 1/4 inch cubes

1 tsp paprika

1 tsp salt

1/2 tsp black pepper

1 green bell pepper, cut into 1/4-inch cubes

cooking spray

Sprinkle half of the salt and pepper over the chicken thighs. Grill on both sides. Let cool and cut into 1/4-inch cubes. Coat a pan with cooking spray and add the onion, bell pepper, and potato. Season with the paprika and the rest of the salt and pepper. Cook over medium heat until tender and brown. Add the chicken and stir. Heat thoroughly.

Servings	Calories	Protein	Carbohydrates	Fat
2	386	42 g	19 g	15 g

Grilled Chicken Tex-Mex

4 skinless, boneless chicken breasts

4 ripe whole tomatoes, chopped

1 small red onion, chopped

2 Tbs cilantro, finely chopped

juice of 2 limes

salt and freshly ground pepper

Lightly salt and pepper both sides of the chicken breasts, then grill until just done. While the chicken is grilling, combine the remaining ingredients in a bowl. Season with salt and pepper and mix well. Serve the chicken with the salsa spooned on top.

Servings	Calories	Protein	Carbohydrates	Fat
2	415	64 g	15 g	10 g

Cooked Down Chicken over Polenta

12 chicken thighs

1 can whole tomatoes, drained, seeded, and chopped

1 oz dried porcine mushrooms

1 tsp nutmeg

1 bay leaf

1 onion, chopped

1/4 cup fresh basil, chopped

1 cup red wine

polenta squares (see recipe on page 172)

salt and pepper

Cover the mushrooms in hot water and let stand until soft. Chop and set aside. Strain the mushroom water through a cheesecloth and set aside. Remove the skin and fat from the chicken thighs, then place them in a saucepan and cover with water. Bring to a boil. Reduce the heat and simmer for 30 minutes, skimming off the froth. Remove the thighs and set aside to cool. Bring the liquid back to boil. Add the onion, tomatoes, mushrooms, basil, bay leaf, red wine, nutmeg, strained mushroom juice, salt, and pepper.

When the chicken is cool enough to handle, remove the meat from the bones and add it to the pot. Continue to boil until all of the liquid has evaporated, stirring occasionally to make sure no food is sticking to the pot. When all of the visible liquid is gone, remove from the heat. Adjust the seasonings to taste, and spoon over polenta squares.

Servings	Calories	Protein	Carbohydrates	Fat
6 (without polenta)	246	28 g	10 g	10 g

Roast Turkey

One of the benefits of living in a free country is not having to wait for Thanksgiving to have a turkey dinner. The makings of a turkey dinner, complete with dressing, gravy, mashed potatoes, and cranberry sauce are available at your local grocery store year-round. Best of all, turkey can easily be made to conform to the bodybuilding and fitness lifestyle. In addition, whole turkeys are economical since the leftovers can be eaten for days afterward.

After much trial and error, I think I have found the roasting method that produces the most moist meat and the best flavor with the least amount of fat. It's so easy to prepare, and tastes so good, that you have little excuse not to enjoy turkey

as often as you wish. There are a few simple rules that you'll need to follow.

Most of the whole turkeys you find in the market between holidays will be frozen. You must take care in defrosting the bird to avoid spoilage. Leaving the turkey out at room temperature to thaw is a sure way to get food poisoning because the outer parts of the bird will become too warm before the whole bird is defrosted. The safest way is to leave the turkey in its packaging and place it on a tray in the refrigerator for 3 or 4 days. If you don't have that much time, soak the turkey, still packaged, in a sink full of cold water. Change the water every half hour. With this method, a rock solid 12-pound bird will be ready to cook in about 6 hours. Microwave defrosting is not recommended because it cooks parts of the bird while other parts remain frozen solid. Once the turkey is defrosted, remove the wrapper, neck, and giblets. Give it a thorough rinsing and pat it dry with paper towels. You must refrigerate or cook the bird immediately.

Traditionally, turkey is stuffed. However, the bird can be cooked for less time and at a lower temperature if you omit stuffing, yielding more moist and tender meat. I opt for this method and prepare the stuffing separately, as a casserole. If you must stuff the bird, wait until just before it goes into the oven. Also, be sure that any meat ingredients used in the stuffing are thoroughly cooked.

Use an instant-read meat thermometer for best results in determining when the turkey is done. Insert the thermometer in the thickest part of the thigh, not touching the bone. The temperature should read 175°F to 180°F for an unstuffed bird. If your bird is stuffed, insert the thermometer into the center of the stuffing through the breast. The turkey will be done when the temperature in the center reads 180°F to 185°F.

The method of roasting a turkey is also a subject of great debate. Once again, having tried all of the popular methods, I will give you the method that I think produces the best finished product. Instead of stuffing the bird, you should place a couple of carrots, a stalk of celery, and a quartered onion in the body cavity. This does not constitute stuffing because the cavity is quite loosely filled and the ends are not sewn up. The steam emanating from the vegetables as they cook will produce a more moist and flavorful bird.

Place the turkey, breast up, on a V-rack in the center of a large roasting pan. Cover the breast with a small tent made of aluminum foil. Roast the turkey in a raging 450°F oven for 30 minutes, then lower the heat to 325°F. Let the turkey roast for the equivalent of 15 minutes per pound before you start checking the internal temperature. During the last half hour, remove the foil tent and baste the bird with the pan juices at 15 minute intervals until done.

Let the turkey stand for 20 minutes, loosely covered with foil, before you carve. This will allow the juices to evenly moisten the meat.

Servings	Calories	Protein	Carbohydrates	Fat
1 lb raw (8 oz cooked)	395	65 g	0 g	13 g

Stuffing

3 Italian turkey sausages, removed from the casings

2 stalks celery, finely chopped

1 onion, finely chopped

1 cup chicken or turkey stock

1 cup white rice (3 cups lightly salted chicken or turkey stock for cooking)

1 cup oyster mushrooms, finely chopped

3 cloves garlic, finely minced

1 tsp sage

1 tsp black pepper

2 tsp salt

2 egg whites

Heat 1/2 cup of water to boiling in a large sauté pan. Reduce the heat to medium-high and add the turkey sausage. Using a wooden spoon, continually stir the meat and break it into small pieces. Once the water is completely evaporated, the meat will begin to fry in the fat rendered during boiling. Continue to stir the meat until it turns brown. Add the garlic, onion, celery, mushrooms, sage, black pepper, and salt. Stir the mixture frequently with a wooden spoon, making sure to scrape up anything that is stuck the bottom of the pan. When the vegetables are soft and most of the liquid has evaporated, remove the pan from the heat and set aside until cool. Cover and refrigerate overnight.

Meanwhile, cook the rice in the stock over medium-high heat. When the stock is down to the level of the rice, cover the pan and remove it from the heat. The rice will continue to absorb the rest of the liquid without burning. Once the pot is cool to the touch, refrigerate overnight.

Remove the mixture from the refrigerator and let sit for about 1 hour, until it reaches room temperature. Combine the pre-cooked ingredients in a large bowl and mix well. Add the egg white and the stock and mix well. Adjust the seasonings to taste.

The stuffing may be put into a room-temperature turkey or cooked in a covered casserole at 325°F for 1 1/2 hours.

Servings	Calories	Protein	Carbohydrates	Fat
4	81	3 g	16 g	0 g

Turkey Gravy

de-fatted pan drippings*

2 cups turkey or chicken stock

1/2 tsp salt

1 Tbs cornstarch

1/4 cup white wine

1 bay leaf

*To de-fat the pan drippings, remove the turkey and roasting rack from the roasting pan and pour the contents into a 2-cup Pyrex measuring cup or fat skimmer (a cup with a spout coming out of the bottom like a small watering can). Using a rubber spatula, scrape out as much of the residue from the pan into the cup. Let sit undisturbed for 15 minutes, or until the fat has separated and risen to the top. Skim the fat off and discard it.

Pour the de-fatted pan drippings into a medium saucepan and bring to a boil over high heat. Add the bay leaf and continue to boil until reduced by half. Strain the liquid through a cheesecloth-lined strainer, return to the pot, and bring back to a boil. Dissolve the cornstarch in the white wine. Remove the pan from the heat and add the cornstarch mixture, stirring constantly. The gravy should thicken immediately. Add the salt and adjust the seasonings to taste.

Servings	Calories	Protein	Carbohydrates	Fat
8	16	0 g	3 g	0 g

Oriental Turkey Thighs

2 turkey thighs, fat trimmed and butterflied (see page 23)

2 green onions, chopped

6 cloves garlic, crushed

1 Tbs fresh ginger, chopped

1/2 cup mirin

1/2 cup low-sodium soy sauce

2 Tbs Dijon mustard

2 Tbs cilantro

Combine all of the ingredients except the turkey in a large bowl and mix well. Immerse the meat in this marinade, then cover and refrigerate for at least 2 hours.

Grill or barbecue the turkey. Any remaining marinade will keep for 1 week in the refrigerator. Slice the turkey and serve with Chinese mustard.

Servings	Calories	Protein	Carbohydrates	Fat
2	479	70 g	12 g	12 g

Turkey Wontons

4 oz ground turkey breast

2 tsp fresh ginger, minced

2 Tbs green onion, finely chopped

1 egg white

2 Tbs low-sodium soy sauce

12 square wonton wrappers

    (available in the refrigerated Oriental section in most supermarkets)

cooking spray

Combine the ground turkey, ginger, green onion, egg white, and soy sauce in a bowl and mix well. Place 1 tablespoon of the mixture in the center of a wrapper. Using a pastry brush or your finger, lightly wet the edges of the wrapper with water. Make a triangular pouch with the filling inside by folding the wrapper diagonally, then squeeze the edges together to seal the pouch. While holding the triangle folded side down, dab a drop of water on the corners. Fold the points over so they meet in the center, and then press the points together to make them stick.

    Coat a metal colander with cooking spray. Arrange the wontons in a single layer covering the bottom of the colander. Boil about 1 inch of water in a saucepan large enough to hold the colander suspended over the water by its rim. Cover and let the wontons steam for about 10 minutes. The wontons may also be cooked in soup.

Servings	Calories	Protein	Carbohydrates	Fat
2	248	20 g	22 g	8 g

Turkey Meat Loaf

2 lbs ground turkey breast

1 envelope Lipton non-fat instant onion soup mix

2 egg whites

1 tsp garlic salt

1 small can tomato paste

cooking spray

Preheat the oven to 350°F. Coat a loaf pan with cooking spray. Combine the first 3 ingredients in a bowl and mix well by squishing the ingredients through your fingers. (There is no kitchen tool that works better for mixing meat loaf than a pair of thoroughly washed bare hands.) Shape the mixture into a ball and press it into the coated loaf pan. Spread the tomato paste over the top of the meat loaf and sprinkle with the garlic salt. Bake for 40 minutes, until a meat thermometer inserted in the center of the loaf registers 185°F.

Servings	Calories	Protein	Carbohydrates	Fat
4	543	62 g	11 g	28 g

Turkey Burgers

1 lb ground turkey breast

1 small onion, finely chopped

1 egg white

1 tsp salt

1/2 tsp pepper

Combine the ingredients in a bowl and mix well using the "hand" method described above. Shape the meat into 4 equal patties and grill or barbecue.

Servings	Calories	Protein	Carbohydrates	Fat
2	510	61 g	3 g	28 g

Chapter Seven

MEAT

B eef, lamb, pork, veal, and game—and their suitability for bodybuilders—have been a subject of great confusion. I'd like to dispel some of the myths.

Myth #1:

"Red meat is very high in calories." That's certainly possible. An 8-ounce porterhouse or T-bone steak has about 900 calories and 70 g of fat. Not exactly diet food. However, an 8-ounce serving of flank steak or eye-of-round, with all visible fat removed, has only about 400 calories and 15 g of fat. Definitely diet food. The protein content of the leaner cut is also higher: 70 g versus 50 g, respectively. The numbers speak for themselves. Lean cuts of beef should definitely be part of a bodybuilder's diet.

M y t h # 2 :

"Pork is the other white meat." Well, if you overcook it, it looks white, but that's about the extent of any similarity to poultry, which is the true white meat. Ounce for ounce, pork contains more marbled (intramuscular) fat than any other meat and is consequently the highest in calories. Pork advocates will argue that the fat content in pork has dropped 25 to 30 percent in the last 5 years. Perhaps, but I've never been able to look at a package of pork at any meat counter and say, "Gee, that looks pretty lean." The leaner cuts have been very tough and very dry. Ham, the cured and smoked hind legs of the pig, can be quite low in fat. However, the smoking process adds tremendous amounts of sodium. So if you want white meat, eat chicken.

M y t h # 3 :

"Red meat is hard to digest and stays in your system for weeks at a time." If you really think about it, how could it? What does the red meat do? Does it leave the digestive tract and hide? In humans, digestion is aided by an involuntary muscle movement called peristalsis, the slow rhythmic rippling of the intestines that moves the food along. Now, I've never performed exploratory surgery on someone who had eaten red meat a few weeks earlier, but if the meat could somehow defy peristalsis and collect in the digestive tract, it would block the intestines. A blocked intestine is dangerous indeed, and quite painful. If not treated properly, the intestine could burst and cause death. Given the tons of red meat consumed in this country each year and the relatively low number of deaths due to intestinal blockage, I think we can safely surmise that eating red meat in moderation is perfectly fine.

Myth #4:

"Red meat is bad for you." Why? Yes, the cattle industry has some interesting ways of inducing cows to grow, but then, so do bodybuilders. Living in New York City isn't good for people either, but its 9 million residents seem to be faring pretty well. If humans were not meant to eat meat, we wouldn't have teeth capable of chewing it or enzymes capable of digesting it.

Myth #5:

"The body will mimic what you feed it. If you want to build muscle you must eat red meat because human muscle is essentially red meat. You must eat protein that looks like your own muscle and lots of it." I've heard this from more people than I can count. This ludicrous "reasoning" may account for the fact that a Butterfinger wrapper and Bart Simpson are the same color, but human anabolic activity just doesn't work that way.

When protein, any protein, is eaten, the body's digestive process breaks down the bonds that hold the protein's amino acid chains together. This allows the protein to enter the body as peptides or individual amino acids. Complete protein chains are far too complex to be absorbed in the intestines. Once broken down to amino acids and absorbed, the body will combine individual amino acids as it needs them to form specific proteins. It doesn't matter what protein the amino acids came from. The body cannot tell the difference between valine from a cow or valine from a soy bean. Valine is valine, period.

There is absolutely no medical literature (and I've read a lot of it) that proves conclusively that eating red meat in moderation is bad for you. Given the arguments for and against it, I believe the pros outweigh the cons by quite a bit. Ultimately, you must choose whether or not to eat red meat. If you do choose to eat meat, you'll find that the recipes in this chapter will make it much more interesting.

B e e f

Of all of the red meats, beef is the most widely consumed. The less you cook it, the more nutritious it is, since overcooking can destroy its nutrient value; specifically amino acids and creatine. Beef should be cooked to an internal temperature of 120°F for rare, 130°F for medium, and 150°F for well done. Grilling or roasting beef will help it to retain its juices and natural flavor. Beef can also be sautéed or stewed for rich, savory dishes. Always choose the leaner cuts, such as eye-of-round and flank steak.

P o r k

If you must eat pork, look for cuts with the least amount of marbled fat. Trim off all external fat, and cook the meat to an internal temperature of at least 180°F. I have not included pork recipes in this book because I maintain that pork is too high in fat to be useful.

L a m b

Lamb is one of my favorite meats. It has a unique flavor and doesn't dry out while cooking. It is also quite high in L-carnitine, an amino acid that helps the mitochondria in muscle cells burn fat.

The leg meat is the best because it contains very little marbled fat and the subcutaneous fat can be easily trimmed away. Lamb is best when grilled and should be cooked to an internal temperature of 135°F to 140°F.

Flank Steak

1 cup dry red wine

1 onion, sliced

1/2 cup red wine vinegar

3 cloves garlic, peeled and split

2 bay leaves

1 tsp salt

1 tsp coarse black pepper

1 8-ounce flank steak

Trim any fat from the flank steak and rub each side with the salt and pepper. Pour the wine and the vinegar into a large baking dish and add the onion, garlic, and bay leaves. Add the meat and turn a few times to coat. Cover the dish with plastic wrap and refrigerate overnight.

Remove the meat from the marinade. Transfer the marinade to a non-stick pan and reduce the liquid by half. Lower the heat and continue to cook until the onions are soft. Meanwhile, grill or barbecue the meat on both sides to desired doneness. Slice thinly across the grain and serve smothered in onions.

Servings	Calories	Protein	Carbohydrates	Fat
1	474	67 g	16 g	16 g

Quick Beef Steak

1 8-ounce lean steak, eye-of-round or other lean cut

1/4 tsp salt

1/4 tsp black pepper

1 clove garlic, finely minced

Pat the steak dry with a paper towel and trim off any fat. Rub both sides with the salt, pepper, and garlic. Grill, broil, or barbecue for 5 to 7 minutes on each side, depending on desired doneness.

Servings	Calories	Protein	Carbohydrates	Fat
1	422	66 g	1 g	15 g

Chili

1 lb lean stew meat, trimmed of excess fat

1 can peeled whole tomatoes, chopped and drained

2 cups beef stock

1 can red pinto beans, rinsed and drained

1 onion, peeled and finely chopped

2 green chili peppers, seeded and chopped

2 red chili peppers, seeded and chopped

3 Tbs chili powder

3 Tbs cornmeal

2 bay leaves

1 tsp cayenne pepper

2 tsp salt

cooking spray

Coat a large saucepan with cooking spray and brown the meat. Add the onions, peppers, bay leaves, cayenne pepper, and salt. Cook over medium heat, stirring occasionally, until the onions begin to soften. Add the tomatoes and beef stock. Bring to a boil, cover partially, and reduce the heat. Simmer for 2 hours, stirring occasionally.   Add the beans and the cornmeal. Stir for 3 to 4 minutes, until thickened. Adjust the seasonings to taste.

Servings	Calories	Protein	Carbohydrates	Fat
4	371	40 g	34 g	9 g

Beef Stew

1 cup Burgundy wine

1 onion, finely chopped

1 lb beef stew meat, trimmed of all fat

2 potatoes, peeled and cut into cubes

3 carrots, peeled, split, and cut into chunks

1 cup pearl onions, peeled and left whole

2 cups beef stock

1 can whole tomatoes, chopped and drained

1 bay leaf

2 Tbs parsley, finely chopped

1 tsp salt

olive-oil-flavored cooking spray

Coat a large saucepan with olive-oil-flavored cooking spray and brown the meat on all sides. Add the tomatoes, onions, beef stock, wine, bay leaf, and salt. Bring to a boil, then reduce the heat. Simmer uncovered for 1 hour, stirring occasionally. If the liquid has not reduced by half, raise the heat and boil away the excess liquid.

Add the remaining vegetables, cover, and cook for about 20 minutes, until tender.

Servings	Calories	Protein	Carbohydrates	Fat
4	341	37 g	25 g	8 g

Meat Loaf

3 egg whites

2 lbs extra lean ground beef (or turkey)

1 onion, finely chopped

2 Tbs fresh parsley, finely chopped

3 cloves garlic, finely chopped

1/2 cup oatmeal

1 cup tomato sauce (see recipe on page 89)

1 cup mushrooms, thinly sliced

2 tsp salt

1 tsp pepper

cooking spray

Preheat the oven to 350°F. Coat a large sauté pan with cooking spray. Add the garlic, onion, mushrooms, and 1 teaspoon of salt. Sauté over medium heat until the onions are soft. Let cool.

Combine the beef and onion mixture with the oatmeal, parsley, remaining teaspoon of salt, pepper, and egg whites in a bowl. Mix well. Coat a loaf pan with cooking spray and press in the meat. Pour the sauce on top and spread evenly. Bake until the internal temperature reaches 130°F. Cool and serve.

Servings	Calories	Protein	Carbohydrates	Fat
6	319	47 g	7 g	10 g

Steak and Peppers

1 8-ounce eye-of-round steak

2 green bell peppers, chopped

1 onion, chopped

1 tsp salt

1 tsp pepper

cooking spray

Sprinkle half of the salt and pepper on both sides of the steak. Grill on both sides to desired doneness. Meanwhile, coat a large sauté pan with cooking spray. Add the onions, peppers, salt, and pepper. Sauté on high heat for about 5 minutes, until the onions are soft. Smother the steak with the onion and pepper mixture and serve.

Servings	Calories	Protein	Carbohydrates	Fat
1	481	68 g	14 g	16 g

Mexican Beef Steak

4 6-ounce rib-eye steaks, all fat removed

cooking spray

1 green pepper, chopped

1 red pepper, chopped

1 onion, chopped

2 Tbs tomato paste

1/2 cup beef stock

1/2 tsp salt

1/8 tsp white pepper

Tabasco sauce to taste

1/2 Tbs tequila or vodka

1/8 tsp cayenne pepper

Coat a sauté pan with cooking spray. Sauté the onions until just brown. Add the peppers and cook for another 2 minutes. Mix the tomato paste with the beef stock and add to the pan. Add the salt, white pepper, and a few drops of Tabasco. Cover and simmer for 10 minutes over medium heat.

Meanwhile, rub both sides of each steak with black pepper and grill to desired doneness. Remove from the grill, cover, and keep warm.

Uncover the vegetables and raise the heat. Add the tequila or vodka and the cayenne pepper. Boil for about 2 minutes to evaporate the alcohol. Adjust the seasonings to taste. Pour the sauce on a large warm platter and arrange the steaks on top.

Servings	Calories	Protein	Carbohydrates	Fat
4	342	50 g	5 g	12 g

Roast Beef

1 4-lb roast, extra lean with fat well trimmed

salt

freshly ground black pepper

Preheat the oven to 450°F. Place the roast on a rack in a roasting pan. Rub the roast thoroughly with salt and pepper. Place the roasting pan on the center rack of the oven and cook for 15 minutes at 450°F. Lower the heat to 375°F and cook for another 30 minutes. Lower the heat to 325°F and cook for another 30 minutes. Check the internal temperature with a meat thermometer, and keep roasting until the temperature reads 120°F. Remove from the oven and cover with aluminum foil. Let stand for 20 minutes before serving. Carve at a slight angle, against the grain.

Servings	Calories	Protein	Carbohydrates	Fat
12	279	44 g	0 g	10 g

Gravy

pan drippings

1 cup beef stock

2 bay leaves

1 Tbs cornstarch

salt and pepper

Remove the fat from the pan drippings. Add the stock and bay leaves. Bring to a boil and reduce the liquid by half. Dissolve the cornstarch in 1/4 cup of cold water. Remove the gravy from the heat and add the cornstarch mixture. Stir until thickened. Season to taste with salt and pepper.

Servings	Calories	Protein	Carbohydrates	Fat
8	9	0 g	2 g	0 g

Oven-Roasted Lamb and Potatoes

1 leg of lamb, boned, trimmed of all fat and cut into chunks

1 large onion, halved and sliced

1 green pepper, seeded and chopped

1 red pepper, seeded and chopped

3 large potatoes, peeled and cut into chunks

1 bay leaf

1/4 tsp dried oregano, crushed

1 tsp salt

1/2 tsp black pepper

olive-oil-flavored cooking spray

Preheat the oven to 375°F. Coat a large roasting pan with olive-oil-flavored cooking spray. Add the lamb chunks, onion, and bell peppers. Season with the remaining ingredients and toss well. Arrange the ingredients evenly in the pan. Bake for about 1 hour, stirring occasionally, until the potatoes are tender. Remove from the oven and discard the bay leaf. Cover with aluminum foil and let rest for 20 minutes before serving.

Servings	Calories	Protein	Carbohydrates	Fat
4	481	66 g	13 g	16 g

Butterflied Leg of Lamb

1 leg of lamb, fat trimmed and butterflied (see page 23)

1 red onion, halved and thinly sliced

1 cup red wine

1 bay leaf

1/4 cup low-sodium soy sauce

1/4 cup balsamic vinegar

2 Tbs Dijon mustard

1 tsp black pepper

Place the meat in a large baking dish. Combine the red wine, vinegar, soy sauce, mustard, and black pepper in a bowl and mix well with a wire whisk. Add the bay leaf and onion. Pour the mixture over the meat. Turn the meat several times to coat, cover with plastic wrap, and refrigerate overnight.

While starting the barbecue, remove the meat from the refrigerator and allow it to come to room temperature. When the coals are ready, remove the meat from the marinade and scrape away the excess. Barbecue the meat on both sides. Remove from the grill, cover with foil, and let rest for 20 minutes before carving.

Meanwhile, empty the marinade into a non-stick sauté pan and reduce the liquid by half. Lower the heat and continue to cook until the onions are very soft.

Carve the meat against the grain in thin slices. Serve with the sautéed onions.

Servings	Calories	Protein	Carbohydrates	Fat
4	433	65 g	4 g	16 g

Grilled Lamb Chops

4 shoulder lamb chops

4 cloves garlic, peeled and crushed

1 1/2 tsp salt

1/2 tsp black pepper

Place the crushed garlic cloves close together in the center of a cutting board and sprinkle the salt over them. Using the flat side of a knife, mash the salt into the garlic to form a fine paste. Pat the lamb chops dry with a paper towel and rub the garlic paste evenly over both sides of each chop. Sprinkle with black pepper and grill on both sides until done.

Servings	Calories	Protein	Carbohydrates	Fat
4	426	65 g	1 g	16 g

Lamb and Rice with Mint

1 lb lamb leg meat, cubed, with fat removed

1 cup basmati rice

1 onion, finely chopped

3 cloves garlic, finely minced

1 medium eggplant, cubed (about 2 cups)

1 tsp salt

1/4 cup fresh mint leaves, finely chopped

4 ripe plum tomatoes, peeled, seeded, and chopped

2 cups beef stock

olive-oil-flavored cooking spray

Coat a large saucepan with olive-oil-flavored cooking spray and brown the meat. (This may have to be done in batches to avoid overcrowding the pot.) Remove the browned meat and set aside. Respray the pot and add the garlic, onion, eggplant, and salt. Sauté over medium heat until all of the liquid rendered from the vegetables boils away and they start to fry. Add the rice and stir to coat. Raise the heat to high. Add the remaining ingredients, including the reserved meat, and stir. When the liquid begins to boil, lower the heat to medium-low, and cover the pot. Continue to cook, covered, for about 15 minutes, until the liquid reaches the level of the rice. Remove from the heat, cover, and let stand for 20 minutes, until all of the liquid has been absorbed.

Servings	Calories	Protein	Carbohydrates	Fat
2	652	72 g	49 g	18 g

Chapter Eight

FISH AND SEAFOOD

Calorie for calorie, fish contains more useable protein than any other food. Fish is also high in vitamins A, B, D, and K, and contains particularly high levels of calcium, iodine, magnesium, phosphorous, potassium, and iron. In addition, fish is low in sodium and cholesterol.

The level of fat in fish varies, but unlike most foods, the types of fish that have the lowest levels of fat also tend to be the best-tasting. Cod, halibut, catfish, haddock, tuna, orange roughy, sole, sea bass, and shellfish all contain less than 5 percent fat.

The higher-fat, usually cold-water, fish such as salmon, sardines, mackerel, and trout, contain high levels of DHA and EPA, essential fatty acids that must be included in the diet. You should eat at least 2 servings per week of these types of fish.

Here's the general rule of thumb to determine the fat content of fish: Higher-fat fish tends to have darker, more distinctively flavored flesh, and doesn't store as long as lean fish. Lean fish has whiter meat, keeps longer (up to a week in the refrigerator), but does have a tendency to dry out when cooked. Of course, with the Muscle Meal recipes, you will never be accused of serving dry fish.

All of the lean types of fish have about the same caloric content: about 110 calories per 4-ounce serving (before cooking). As this is obviously much lower than beef or chicken, you can opt for fish as often as you'd like.

Poaching

Fish can easily be destroyed by overcooking. Assiduous attention to cooking time should supersede all attempts to glamorize the fish. Since fish contains very little fat, overcooking results in small, dried out fish. What once started out as a healthy 8-ounce portion can quickly lose 30 or 40 percent of its original bulk. Is there anyone out there who would be satisfied with less? I don't think so.

Perhaps the best method of cooking fish to ensure moistness and size is poaching. Broiling, baking, and grilling use so much heat that the fish can dehydrate after just a few moment's inattention. Remember, fish needs very little cooking time. If it's fresh enough, it can be eaten raw. However, if sashimi reminds you more of bait than the substance of a meal, poaching is the next best alternative.

Poaching is defined as a method of cooking food in a small amount of boiling or simmering liquid. The liquid can be any combination of wine, fish stock, or water. The cooking time can be determined by following the simple "10 minutes per inch" rule: For each inch of thickness allow 10 minutes of cooking time.

For example, let's say you have a beautiful 1 1/2 inch thick whitefish fillet. Estimate the amount of liquid needed to cover the fish, and add it to a deep pan wide enough to hold the fillet. Bring the liquid to a boil, then lower the heat to a slow rolling boil and gently immerse the fillet. Cover with a piece of wax paper and poach for 15 minutes (1.5 inches x 10 minutes). Remove the fillet with a slotted spoon and it's ready to serve. It's that simple! The fillet is plump and tender and you haven't added a single drop of fat. Most importantly, the fish has retained most of its original size.

Poaching is not only optimal, but foolproof. This is not to say that broiling, baking, and grilling should be cast aside. On the contrary, anything that breeds variety is okay, especially on a diet. But if you do choose one of the other methods, be prepared to man your post at the stove vigilantly. Do not leave to answer the phone, watch that incredible shot on instant replay, or finish the article you were reading in Muscular Development. Chances are that the 8-dollar-a-pound fillet you're tending will end up re-engineering its molecules——into something resembling coal. Even if you're careful, you'll still need to test the fish to make sure it is done. There is no foolproof rule of thumb for these other cooking methods.

As the fish approaches what you think may be its final cooking time, insert a fork into the thickest part of the fillet and gently try to pull it apart. If the meat pulls away easily in large flakes, it's done. If not, give it 2 or 3 more minutes and try again. You will be amazed at how quickly it cooks. Once you have success with each of these methods, your estimate of cooking time will become more accurate. Until then, your fillets may end up in several pieces.

These methods work for all fish, not just the low-fat varieties. Since uniform cuts cook more evenly, fillets and steaks are more predictable than whole fish.

Once the fish is cooked, it can be eaten a variety of non-fat sauces, or just a squeeze of lemon. The fish sauce recipes I've included don't have to be restricted to fish. They wake up a plain chicken breast, turkey patty, or steamed vegetables just as well. As always, feel free to use your imagination.

Mock Lemon Herb Butter Sauce

1 cup poaching liquid

1/2 tsp dried tarragon

1 Tbs cornstarch

1 tsp Butter Buds

1/4 tsp salt

1/4 cup dry white wine

juice of 1 lemon

Bring the poaching liquid to a boil in a small saucepan. Add the tarragon, lemon juice, and Butter Buds. Reduce the liquid by half.

Dissolve the cornstarch in the wine. Remove the pan from the heat. Add the salt and stir in the cornstarch mixture. Continue to stir as the sauce thickens. Spoon over poached fish. This sauce feels and tastes like it contains butter, but it doesn't. So pour it on!

Servings	Calories	Protein	Carbohydrates	Fat
8	11	0 g	2 g	0 g

Dijon Lime Sauce

2 Tbs Dijon mustard

1 Tbs fresh cilantro, chopped

2 tsp low-sodium soy sauce

1 tsp garlic salt

juice of 2 limes

Combine all of the ingredients in a small bowl and mix well with a wire whisk. Spoon over poached fish.

Servings	Calories	Protein	Carbohydrates	Fat
4	13	0 g	1 g	1 g

Chinese Fish Sauce

1/4 cup low-sodium soy sauce

1 Tbs oyster sauce (found in the Oriental section of your supermarket)

1 tsp fresh ginger, finely minced

1 Tbs green onion, finely chopped

Combine all of the ingredients in a small bowl and mix well with a wire whisk. Spoon over poached fish.

Servings	Calories	Protein	Carbohydrates	Fat
4	13	0 g	1 g	0 g

Basil Garlic Sauce

1 cup poaching liquid

1/4 cup fresh basil leaves, chopped

1 clove garlic, peeled

1/2 tsp salt

Bring the poaching liquid to a boil in small saucepan and reduce by 2/3. Cool slightly and pour into a blender. Add the remaining ingredients and pulse until smooth. Pour over poached fish.

Servings	Calories	Protein	Carbohydrates	Fat
8	2	0 g	0 g	0 g

Tuna Salad

1 6 oz can albacore tuna, packed in water

1 small red onion, halved and thinly sliced

1 rib celery, finely sliced

2 Tbs balsamic vinegar

1 Tbs lemon juice

1/4 tsp black pepper

Drain the tuna and combine with the onion and celery in a small bowl. In another bowl, whisk together the vinegar, lemon juice, and black pepper. Pour over the tuna and mix well.

Servings	Calories	Protein	Carbohydrates	Fat
1	221	40 g	9 g	0 g

Steamed Oriental Sea Bass

4 8-ounce sea bass fillets

4 green onions, shredded

1/2 cup rice vinegar

2 Tbs fermented black bean paste (found in Oriental markets)

1 Tbs fresh ginger, sliced

Combine the rice vinegar, ginger, and enough water to fill the bottom of a steamer or large saucepan with 2 inches of liquid. Arrange the fish on steaming tray or large plate. Spread the black bean paste over the fillets and top with the shredded green onion. Bring the liquid to a boil. Place the fish on a rack 1 inch above the liquid. Cover and steam for 10 to 20 minutes, until the fish pulls away in large flakes.

Servings	Calories	Protein	Carbohydrates	Fat
4	228	44 g	3 g	3 g

Sea Bass with Tomato and Fennel

1 can whole tomatoes, seeded, chopped, and drained

2 onions, halved and thinly sliced

1 cup dry white wine

2 cups fish stock

juice of 1 lemon

1 lb sea bass fillets

1 cup fennel, finely chopped

1 bay leaf

salt and pepper

Preheat the oven to 350°F. In a roasting pan, combine the tomatoes, onions, white wine, stock, and lemon juice. Bring to a boil on the stove and cook for about 10 minutes, until the onions start to soften. Turn off the heat.

Sprinkle the fillets with salt and pepper and sink them into the tomato and onion mixture. Add the fennel and bay leaf. Cover the pan with foil and bake for 20 minutes. Remove the cover, raise the heat to 425°F, and bake for another 10 minutes.

Gently remove the fish from pan and place on a serving platter. Cover and set aside. Pour the contents of the roasting pan into a saucepan, remove the bay leaf, and reduce the liquid by half. Pour the sauce over the fish and serve.

Servings	Calories	Protein	Carbohydrates	Fat
4	190	25 g	19 g	2 g

Shark Kabobs

1 lb shark steaks, cut in 1-inch cubes

1 lb cherry tomatoes

1 lb large mushrooms

1 large onion, quartered and cut into 1-inch slices and separated

1/2 cup low-sodium soy sauce

2 Tbs lemon juice

1 Tbs honey

Soak the skewers in water for 1 hour to keep them from burning.

Alternately skewer the onion, shark, tomato, and mushrooms. Set aside.

In a small bowl, whisk together the soy sauce, lemon juice, and honey. Broil or grill the kabobs on all sides, basting with the liquid, for about 15 minutes, until the shark is done.

Servings	Calories	Protein	Carbohydrates	Fat
4	229	26 g	18 g	5 g

Haddock and Basmati Rice

1 lb haddock

1 cup basmati rice

5 1/2 cups fish stock

1 onion

1/2 tsp turmeric

1 tsp gara marsala

2 Tbs cornstarch or arrowroot

1 bay leaf

1 tsp salt

cooking spray

Poach the haddock in the fish stock according to the thickness rule (see pages 148-149). Set aside. Skim any froth from the stock. Remove 2 1/2 cups of the stock and set aside. Reduce the remaining stock by 2/3, so there is 1 cup left. Set aside.

Coat a saucepan with cooking spray. Chop the onion and add it to the pan with the salt, turmeric, gara marsala, and black pepper. Sauté until the onion turns opaque. Add the rice and cook for 3 minutes, until the rice starts to become more opaque. Add the 2 1/2 cups of reserved stock and the bay leaf. Cover, reduce the heat, and cook for about 20 minutes, until all of the liquid is absorbed. Remove from the heat.

Reheat the reduced stock. Dissolve 2 tablespoons of cornstarch or arrowroot in 1/4 cup of water. Just as the stock boils, remove it from the heat and add the cornstarch mixture. Stir until thickened. Remove the bay leaf from the rice and add the fish pieces and sauce. Stir to incorporate.

Servings	Calories	Protein	Carbohydrates	Fat
2	385	46 g	42 g	2 g

Fish Stew

2 cups white wine

1 lb white fleshy fish like sea bass, haddock, or catfish, cut into 1-inch cubes

10 mussels

10 clams

8 oz medium shrimp, peeled and deveined

1 can whole tomatoes, chopped and drained

2 medium carrots, peeled and cut in 1-inch pieces

3 potatoes, peeled and cut in 1-inch cubes

1 large onion, finely chopped

2 ribs celery, finely sliced

2 Tbs flat Italian parsley, finely chopped

olive-oil-flavored cooking spray

2 Tbs lemon juice

6 cups fish stock

salt and pepper

Coat a large saucepan with olive-oil-flavored cooking spray and add the onion, celery, and salt. Sauté for 4 to 5 minutes, until the onion turns opaque. Add the tomatoes, potatoes, carrots, parsley, and fish stock. Bring to a boil and continue boiling until the liquid is reduced by half.

In the meantime, clean the clams and mussels and place them in a large stock pot. Pour in the wine and bring to a boil. Cover and cook over high heat for 5 to 10 minutes, just until the shells open. Remove from the heat and let cool until you can handle the shells. Remove the meat from the shells and reserve in a covered bowl. Discard the shells along with any unopened clams or mussels.

Pour the remaining cooking liquid through a cheesecloth-lined strainer directly into the reduced contents of the first saucepan. Bring to a boil and reduce by 1/3. Add the fish cubes and cook for another 10 minutes, stirring occasionally. Add the shrimp and cook for another 5 minutes. Add the shucked clams and adjust the seasonings to taste.

Servings	Calories	Protein	Carbohydrates	Fat
4	372	47 g	34 g	3 g

Whitefish Salad

1 lb whitefish
juice of 2 lemons, strained
1 tsp extra virgin olive oil
1/4 cup chopped flat Italian parsley
salt and pepper

Poach the whitefish in slowly boiling water according to the thickness rule (see pages 148-149). Drain and spread out on a plate to cool. In a small bowl, add the lemon juice and whisk in the olive oil, salt, pepper, and parsley. Pour over the cooled fish. Refrigerate until cold. Toss well and serve.

Servings	Calories	Protein	Carbohydrates	Fat
2	322	44 g	6 g	13 g

Hot Snapper Salad

1 lb red snapper

2 or 3 tomatoes, chopped

1 clove garlic, finely minced

1 jalapeño pepper, finely chopped

1/3 cup lemon juice

1 Tbs cilantro

salt and pepper

Poach the red snapper in slowly boiling water or stock according to the thickness rule (see pages 148-149). Drain and let cool. Cut the fish into small cubes and combine with the remaining ingredients in a large bowl. Mix well.

Servings	Calories	Protein	Carbohydrates	Fat
2	280	49 g	13 g	4 g

Shellfish

Shellfish is probably one of the most misunderstood items on the food chain. I can't begin to count the number of arguments I've been lured into over whether shellfish—crab, clams, mussels, lobster, oysters, scallops, and shrimp—can be part of a healthy diet. I've heard all kinds of antiquated theories and old wives' tales— everything from its reputed high cholesterol content to its potential health hazards—without any documentation to back up the allegations.

I'm here to tell you that if you like shellfish, you should dig in to your heart's content. With the exception of shrimp and crab, shellfish's cholesterol content is

comparable to cod, halibut, and tuna. Shrimp and crab are a bit higher, roughly equal to lean beef and turkey. On the whole, as the following table illustrates, shellfish is very low in fat.

Food	Serving	Calories	Protein	Carbs	Fat	Cholesterol
crab	3 oz	100	15 g	2 g	>1 g	85 mg
clams	3 oz	65	11 g	2 g	1 g	55 mg
mussels	3 oz	70	12 g	2 g	>1 g	45 mg
lobster	3 oz	77	14 g	>1 g	>1 g	57 mg
oysters	3 oz	80	10 g	4 g	2 g	40 mg
scallops	3 oz	69	13 g	>1 g	>1 g	30 mg
shrimp	3 oz	100	21 g	1 g	1 g	96 mg

Sources: Nutrition, Concepts and Controversies, 3rd edition (Hamilton, Whitney, Sizer), Nutrition Almanac, 2nd edition (Kirschmann, Dunne), Basic Nutrition and Diet Therapy (Williams)

Compare these to the values for other common protein sources. You'll have to agree that shellfish is a respectable addition to a healthy diet.

Food	Serving	Calories	Protein	Carbs	Fat	Cholesterol
cod	3 oz	66	15 g	0 g	>1 g	72 mg
halibut	3 oz	85	18 g	0 g	>1 g	51 mg
tuna (in water)	3 oz	117	26 g	0 g	>1 g	56 mg
chicken breast	3 oz	100	20 g	0 g	1 g	51 mg
turkey breast	3 oz	150	28 g	0 g	3 g	65 mg
beef (eye-of-round)	3 oz	160 g	25 g	0 g	3 g	77 mg

Sources: Nutrition, Concepts and Controversies, 3rd edition (Hamilton, Whitney, Sizer), Nutrition Almanac, 2nd edition (Kirschmann, Dunne)

The cholesterol and fat content of both groups is quite low considering that one single egg yolk contains 240 mg of cholesterol and 6 g of fat! Food in either category can add a great deal of variety to your diet.

Shellfish cooking is an art form encompassing a vast number of recipes that reach deep into the ethnic background of most European cultures. Countless epic-length cookbooks have been devoted to the cause——and almost all of the recipes contain excessive fat. It pains me to order a 20-dollar plate of scampi in a restaurant and see the little crustaceans brought to me swimming in 15 dollars worth of oil. Somehow, shellfish has become tightly associated with melted butter. Perhaps this is why people unjustly accuse shellfish of having a high cholesterol content.

Despite these misconceptions, shellfish can be delicious sans grease. Shellfish have a delicate array of subtle flavors that are only masked by heavy sauces and melted chub.

The following are a few of the techniques that I frequently employ to prepare shellfish. Because the number of variations is so diverse, I'll only give a brief overview of each method. Use your imagination to discover what works for you and your palate.

C l a m s   a n d   M u s s e l s

Clams are by far the most popular of the shellfish, and happily one of the easiest to prepare. Cleaning is the most time-consuming part of their preparation. Before being scooped up, these little critters spent much of their day buried in mud. Consequently, they are notorious for harboring a great deal of sand and fragments of unidentifiable marine plant life. Giving them a good once over with a firm bristle brush under cold running water is usually all you need to do to get them clean.

Unlike clams, mussels sometimes have what's been termed a "beard" of residual plant life attached to the inside of the mussel and running out through the open end of the shell. A firm tug from the hinge of the shell should completely separate the seaweed from the mussel and leave the flesh intact.

If you run across shellfish that won't close and stay closed while cleaning, toss them. Clams and mussels must be cooked alive; consuming one that has been dead for any length of time can be the cause of an intestinal nightmare you won't soon forget.

Once cleaned and certified living, they are ready to be cooked. The most widely accepted cooking method is steaming. Add just a touch of liquid to start them stewing in their own juice. For a large pot full of either type of shellfish, you only need about 1 cup of liquid——white wine, fish stock, chicken stock, clam juice, or plain water. Simply bring the liquid of your choice to a boil in a large pot and add the shellfish. (If you like, you can add some chopped garlic, shallots, herbs, or tomato sauce.) Cover the pot and steam for 5 to 10 minutes, until the shells open. Remove the pot from the heat and remove the cover immediately. Shellfish overcook rather quickly, leaving the meat dry and rubbery.

Remove the shellfish from the pot and bring the liquid back to a boil. Reduce the liquid by 3/4 and strain it through a very fine strainer. Season to taste. Use the sauce for dipping instead of melted butter.

Crab and Lobster

Once again, simplicity is the key to success in cooking. Because the meat and juices are sealed inside the shell, the result will be the same whether you boil, broil, or barbecue: raising the temperature inside the shell will cause the juice to boil and steam the meat. I like to steam shellfish in some kind of liquid to ensure that the meat doesn't dry out.

Like clams and mussels, crabs and lobsters need to be cooked while still kicking. While you might think this would make scrubbing a bit difficult, a generous dousing with the sprayer in your sink will usually do the trick.

Bring about 2 cups of the cooking liquid of your choice to a boil in a large saucepan and add the cleaned shellfish. Once the liquid returns to a boil, cover the pot and steam for 10 minutes per pound. Remove the cooked shellfish and reduce the liquid to use for dipping. A squeeze of lemon either directly in the reduced cooking liquid or on the shelled meat will enhance the flavor without adding any fat.

Shrimp

There are more ways to cook shrimp than I can count, but only a few enhance their flavor rather than mask it. Because the majority of the flavor is in the shell, shrimp should be peeled before cooking. Use the shells to develop the stock (which will eventually become the sauce). Cooking shrimp with the shell on is a waste of flavor, and it can be annoying to have to peel them before you eat them. In addition, everyone around you will know what you've eaten from the shrimpy odor that you will not be able to scrub off of your fingers.

To remove the shell, simply slice the back of the shrimp along its length, cutting through the shell and about 1/4 of the way through the shrimp. Discard the shell and the digestive tract. Rinse the shrimp under cold running water.

The accumulated shells from 1 pound of shrimp will require 1 cup of liquid for rendering. You can use white wine, fish stock, chicken stock, or water. Whichever you choose, bring it to a boil and add the shells along with 1 bay leaf, 2 cloves of garlic, a few black peppercorns, one shallot, and a sprig of parsley. Lower the heat to barely a simmer and cook the shells for 20 minutes. Strain the liquid through a very fine strainer, pressing out every last drop. Then bring the liquid back to a boil and reduce by half.

Shrimp stock can be the basis for any sauce for grilled, broiled, or steamed shrimp. For example, you can mix 1/4 cup of stock with 1 tablespoon of honey and 2 teaspoons of soy sauce. Brush the mixture on skewered shrimp while they grill. Or, bring 1/2 cup of stock to a boil and add 1 tablespoon of oyster sauce, 1 teaspoon of soy sauce, 1 tablespoon of sweet cooking sherry, 1 teaspoon of finely minced ginger, and 1 tablespoon of chopped cilantro. Add raw shrimp and cook for about 5 minutes, until tender. Pour over rice or Chinese noodles. You could try adding 1/4 cup of stock to each 1/2 cup of Marinara sauce as it cooks. Once the sauce thickens, add the raw shrimp and cook through. Serve over pasta. Shrimp stock can be also added to fish soups and stews to enhance the flavor, whether shrimp will be included in the dish or not.

Oysters and Scallops

Oysters and scallops are the most delicately flavored of all shellfish, and taste best when left alone. A squeeze of lemon or lime is all that's needed to flavor them. Raw scallops and oysters can be added to fish soups and stews; they will poach during the final minutes of cooking. Be careful not to overcook them, as they only take 5 or 6 minutes to cook.

Oysters and scallops are also excellent additions to omelets, casseroles, and quiche. Although not as versatile as the other shellfish, incorporating them into your cooking can provide a unique twist of flavor to otherwise bland dishes. As always, you're only limited by your imagination.

Chapter Nine

BIG FOOD FOR BIG APPETITES

*P*erhaps the greatest challenge I've encountered while preparing a bodybuilder for competition has been to create a diet that allows just enough calories to survive the severe training and aerobic schedule, yet satiates the inevitable hunger pangs that would otherwise lead the frustrated dieter straight to Ben and Jerry's.

There has been no greater test of this acumen than the 7 months I endured helping my wife, Shelley Beattie, to secure a position among the top three Ms. Olympia contenders. Far be it for me to malign my betrothed by disclosing my searches for cookie crumbs in the folds of her car seat, my padlock on the refrigerator, or my attempts to convince her that she would continue to live if she waited another 1/2 hour to eat. I will say this: the woman has an appetite.

Granted, I am quite demanding, especially when I see the kind of great potential that I saw in Shelley. No matter what rigors I put her through, she rose to the occasion and worked her ass off, literally. Sometimes, she hated me in the process.

I trained with her, dieted with her, and did all of the aerobics with her—to no avail. Looking over my shoulder during one of our many afternoon bike rides along the beach, I was sure to see her meandering behind, delirious with hunger, the look of a Freddy Krueger ready to hack me to pieces in her eyes. No amount of discussion meant a hill of beans to her—unless, of course, she could eat it.

No matter how I tried, I could not understand the insatiability of her appetite. I knew it had to be in her head. I'm at least 50 pounds heavier, and although I ate the same measly 1500 calories a day, I came nowhere close to matching her 5 packs of sugar-free gum a day. (Try sharing the same space with someone ingesting that much sorbitol; talk about an olfactory nightmare!) My energy level was fine and I didn't harbor the slightest inclination to cheat.

I had to figure something out, but quick. Although she felt hungrier than I, her weight was coming off at a perfectly calculated half pound per week. I just couldn't give her more food. Her calories had to stay the same.

The solution dawned on me one morning while watching Graham Kerr whip egg whites on the Discovery Channel: Volume! That was the answer. The eyes could fool the stomach. I quickly went to work discovering ways to add volume and texture to the foods we were allowed to eat. Meals could take up more space on the plate and in her stomach, yet not add a single calorie. What a concept: eat air, feel satisfied. It worked! The days leading up to the Ms. Olympia contest became far more tolerable for both of us.

I dedicate the following recipes to Shelley Beattie. Not because she drove me nuts every day with a barrage of complaints too numerous to list, but because she met each day's challenges with the spirit of a champion. She persevered, undaunted by fatigue or disdain for a diet that lasted for 7 months, in her own personal battle to sculpt her body into something the judges would finally notice. Her persistence inspired me to do whatever I could to facilitate her journey, and the following recipes are the result. If a long-term diet is in your future, the Shelley Beattie volume series could be the deciding factor in keeping the men in white suits from making regular stops at your house.

Cornmeal

This is amazing stuff. It's extremely expandable——just add more water. Each ounce of dry cornmeal contains just 100 calories, and 3 ounces cooked in 2 cups of lightly salted water or chicken stock makes a fairly large serving. It can be expanded even further by increasing the cooking liquid.

Cornmeal can also be added to low-calorie soups and stews to thicken them into satisfying meals.

Basic Cornmeal Mush (Polenta)

3 oz dry cornmeal

2 cups water

1 tsp salt

Bring the water to a rolling boil in a 2-quart saucepan and add the salt. Slowly drizzle the cornmeal into the boiling water, stirring constantly with a wire whisk. Reduce the heat to the lowest setting and continue to stir until the mixture thickens. Cook for 5 minutes, stirring constantly. Remove from the heat, cover, and let stand for 10 minutes. Sweetened with Equal and flavored with cinnamon and vanilla extract, this makes a great breakfast. Or, you can make polenta squares.

Polenta Squares

Coat a loaf pan with cooking spray. Pour in the cooked cornmeal, cover with plastic wrap, and set aside for 1 hour. As the cornmeal cools, it becomes solid. It can then be removed from the pan, sliced, and fried in a pan coated with cooking spray. The fried cornmeal can be served with maple syrup for breakfast or with my non-fat tomato sauce as an accompaniment to a meal.

Servings	Calories	Protein	Carbohydrates	Fat
1	300	2 g	71 g	1 g

Extra Thick Chili

8 oz ground turkey meat

cooking spray

3 cloves garlic, crushed and finely chopped

2 Tbs chili powder

1 medium onion, chopped

1 green chili, chopped

1 bay leaf

1 can whole peeled tomatoes, chopped and drained

1 cup chicken stock

1 tsp salt

1/2 tsp freshly ground black pepper

2 oz yellow cornmeal

Coat a large saucepan with cooking spray and brown the meat. Add the garlic, onion, chili powder, green chili, bay leaf, salt, and pepper. Sauté over medium heat until the onions are soft and starting to turn brown. Add the tomatoes and chicken stock and let the mixture simmer for about 20 minutes, stirring occasionally. Remove the bay leaf. Add the cornmeal and stir until the chili thickens. Remove from the heat, cover, and let stand for 10 minutes before serving.

Servings	Calories	Protein	Carbohydrates	Fat
2	490	36 g	56 g	16 g

Egg Whites

Beaten egg whites are perhaps the most effective way to add volume to your meals. To use them wisely, there are a few things you need to know.

First, to ensure maximum volume, the egg whites must be beaten to a point where dipping the beater in and out of the bowl will leave stiff, raised peaks. Some experts contend that greater volume can be achieved by beating the egg whites in a copper-lined bowl. I don't think the extra 10 percent or so of volume is justified by the expense, but if you do, you should spring for the copper bowl. You can find one in any kitchen shop for about 80 bucks.

Second, here's a great trick to stabilize the egg whites and keep them from deflating after they are beaten: when the eggs are three-quarters beaten, sprinkle 1 tablespoon of cornstarch for every 6 egg whites. Then continue to beat to stiff peaks.

Finally, incorporating beaten egg whites into a recipe will require additional cooking time and a slightly lower cooking temperature. These adjustments are necessary to keep the finished product from "falling" as it cools.

The following recipes are some of Shelley's and my favorites.

Breakfast Cake

6 egg whites, beaten to stiff peaks with 1 Tbs cornstarch.

1 cup flour

1 cup non-fat milk

12 packets Sweet One sweetener

2 Tbs vanilla extract

1 tsp salt

1 tsp baking powder

cooking spray

Preheat the oven to 325°F. Coat a 9-inch cake pan with cooking spray. Combine the dry ingredients in a bowl. Add the milk and vanilla and mix well. Add 1/4 of the beaten egg whites and stir to loosen the mixture. Using a rubber spatula, gently fold the remaining egg whites into the batter. Transfer immediately to the coated cake pan.

Bake for 40 to 50 minutes or until a toothpick inserted in the center comes out clean. Let the cake cool slightly in the pan, then invert it over a wire rack. Remove the pan and let the cake cool completely.

You don't have to eat the whole cake, but if you do, you will still be on your diet. You can create endless variations using this cake as a base. For example, split the cake into 2 layers and add Cool Whip Light and strawberries for a low-calorie strawberry shortcake. Or, mix up a batch of sugar-free pudding using non-fat milk and layer the cake with the pudding. However you use it, it beats the pants off a bowl of oatmeal, and will go far toward keeping you sane on your diet.

Servings	Calories	Protein	Carbohydrates	Fat
2	296	16 g	55 g	1 g

Pancakes

6 egg whites, beaten to stiff peaks with 1 Tbs cornstarch
1 cup Hungry Jack instant pancake mix
1 cup water
cooking spray

In a bowl, combine the pancake mix with the water until smooth. Stir 1/4 of the egg whites into the batter to loosen. Using a rubber spatula, fold in the remaining egg whites.

Coat a griddle with cooking spray and heat. Use 1/3 cup of batter per pancake.

Servings	Calories	Protein	Carbohydrates	Fat
2	319	14 g	57 g	4 g

Although I'd prefer that you make your own pancakes from scratch using the recipe on page 183, I do understand the need for convenience. Egg whites can add volume to both recipes. If you do make the pancakes from scratch, follow the same procedure for incorporating the egg whites.

Volume Quiche

6 egg whites

1 cup non-fat milk

3 slices turkey ham, finely cubed

3 oz non-fat cheese, finely cubed

1/2 onion, diced

1/2 pasilla pepper, diced

6 mushrooms, diced

salt and pepper

cooking spray

Preheat the oven to 375°F. Beat the egg whites and milk together in a bowl. Add the turkey ham and cheese. Coat a sauté pan with cooking spray. Add the onions, mushrooms, pasilla pepper, and salt and pepper. Sauté until the ingredients are very dry. Coat a 9-inch pie pan with cooking spray. Spread the vegetable mixture evenly over the bottom. Pour the egg mixture over the vegetables. Bake for 45 minutes.

Servings	Calories	Protein	Carbohydrates	Fat
1	446	59 g	39 g	8 g

C h a p t e r   T e n

BREADS, PIZZA CAKES AND MUFFINS

Meringue

Meringue is an unusual way to eat egg whites, but it's my favorite. It doesn't take much effort, and you do get quite a pile of food to eat.

6 egg whites
2 Tbs sugar
8 packets Sweet One sweetener
1 Tbs cornstarch

Preheat the oven to 325°F. Beat the egg whites to very soft peaks and add the remaining ingredients. Continue to beat to stiff peaks. Transfer the beaten egg whites to a pastry bag fitted with the largest round tip the bag will accommodate.

Line a cookie sheet with parchment or wax paper. Pipe the egg whites into a circle (forming a doughnut shape) until all of the egg whites are used, creating a large, uniform disk. Bake for 1 hour. Let cool and serve.

This meringue disk can be used as the base for a variety of low-calorie desserts or eaten just the way it is.

Servings	Calories	Protein	Carbohydrates	Fat
1	182	14 g	31 g	0 g

Banana Bread

1 ripe banana

2 egg whites

15 packets Sweet One sweetener

1 cup flour

1 tsp baking powder

1 tsp baking soda

2 Tbs non-fat plain yogurt

1/2 tsp grated nutmeg

cooking spray

Preheat the oven to 350°F. Beat the egg whites with the sweetener until foamy and thick. Mash the banana in a food processor. Add to the egg whites. Mix well with a wire whisk. Add the remaining ingredients and just enough water to produce a stiff batter. Coat a loaf pan with cooking spray and pour in the batter. Bake for 30 to 40 minutes, until the bread is golden and a toothpick inserted in the center comes out clean.

Servings	Calories	Protein	Carbohydrates	Fat
16	36	1 g	8 g	0 g

Applesauce Oatmeal Yogurt Muffins

1 1/2 cups rolled oats

1 1/4 cups flour

1 Tbs cinnamon

1 tsp baking powder

1 tsp baking soda

1 cup applesauce

1 cup non-fat plain yogurt

1/3 cup non-fat milk

12 packets Sweet One sweetener

1 egg white

1/2 cup white raisins

cooking spray

Preheat the oven to 400°F. Combine the dry ingredients in a mixing bowl. In a separate bowl, whisk together the yogurt, egg whites, and milk until well blended. Add this mixture to the dry ingredients and mix well. Coat two 6-muffin tins with cooking spray. Fill with batter until within 1/4 inch of the top of each hole. Bake until brown.

Servings	Calories	Protein	Carbohydrates	Fat
12	83	2 g	18 g	0 g

Pancakes

3/4 cup flour

1 egg white

4 tsp baking powder

1 tsp vanilla

6 packets Sweet One sweetener

1/2 cup non-fat milk

1/4 cup non-fat yogurt

1 tsp baking soda

1 tsp white vinegar

Beat the egg white and sweetener together in a mixing bowl. Add the milk and yogurt. Gradually add the flour, beating with a wire whisk until smooth. Add the baking soda, baking powder, and vanilla. Mix well and let stand for 15 minutes.

Coat a griddle with cooking spray and heat. Use 1/3 cup of batter per pancake.

Servings	Calories	Protein	Carbohydrates	Fat
2	220	10 g	42 g	0 g

Corn Muffins

1/2 cup all-purpose flour

1/2 cup cornmeal

1 cup creamed corn

4 tsp baking powder

2 egg whites

10 packets Sweet One sweetener

1/3 cup non-fat milk

1/2 tsp salt

2 tsp vanilla

cooking spray

Preheat the oven to 375°F. Mix all of the ingredients together in a bowl. Beat with a wire whisk until smooth. Coat two 6-muffin pans with cooking spray. Fill with batter until within 1/4 inch of the top of each hole. Bake for 30 to 40 minutes, until golden brown.

Servings	Calories	Protein	Carbohydrates	Fat
12	66	2 g	14 g	0 g

B r e a d

Basing your yeast breads on a starter or sponge will make them more lively, chewy, full-bodied, and flavorful. Sponges are quite easy to prepare and will make a tremendous difference in the finished product.

Sponge

1 cup warm water (about 110°F)
1 Tbs honey
2 packets yeast
2 cups bread flour

In a large mixing bowl, dissolve the honey in the warm water and add the yeast. Moisten the yeast by swishing it around quickly with your finger. Let the mixture sit undisturbed for 3 to 4 minutes, until the yeast bubbles up.

Add the flour and mix with a wire whisk until all of the lumps are gone and the mixture forms a thick batter. Cover with plastic wrap and leave undisturbed in a warm place (an unheated oven is great) for 5 hours or more. The longer the mixture sits, the better.

Whole Wheat Berry Bread

1 sponge
1 cup cooked wheat berries
2 cups whole wheat flour
2 tsp salt
cooking spray

In the bowl of an electric mixer, combine the sponge, wheat berries, and salt. Using a paddle, with the mixer on low speed, add enough flour to form a soft wet dough. Beat the dough on high speed for 3 to 5 minutes. Reduce the speed to low and slowly add enough flour to make the dough pull away from the sides of the bowl and ball up around the paddle.

Turn the mixer off and scrape the dough back into the bowl with a rubber spatula. Replace the paddle with a dough hook and knead the dough for 3 to 5 minutes, adding just enough flour to keep it from sticking.

Turn the dough out onto a lightly floured work surface and knead about 3 or 4 more turns to coat with flour. Mold the dough into a ball. Return the dough to a clean mixing bowl, cover with plastic wrap, and let rise in a warm place for about 3 hours, until it has doubled in volume.

Coat 3 loaf pans with cooking spray. Punch down the dough and scrape it out onto a floured work surface. Knead for 3 to 4 turns and divide it into 3 equal pieces. Place the pieces into the coated loaf pans. Cover with a towel and let the dough rise in a warm place for about 3 hours, until it has doubled in volume again.

Preheat the oven to 350°F. Slit the top of each of the loaves with a very sharp knife or razor blade. Bake on the center rack of the oven for 40 to 50 minutes, until golden brown. Immediately remove the bread from the pans and let cool on a wire rack.

Servings	Calories	Protein	Carbohydrates	Fat
48	30	1 g	6 g	0 g

Italian Cornbread

Unlike Southern cornbread, Italian cornbread is coarse, full of air bubbles, and very chewy.

1 sponge

1 can creamed corn

3 tsp salt

1 1/2 cups yellow cornmeal

1 1/2 cups bread flour

cooking spray

Combine the first 2 ingredients in the bowl of an electric mixer. With the mixer on low, alternately add the cornmeal and flour a little at a time until a very soft wet dough forms. Turn the mixer on high and beat for 3 to 5 minutes.

Coat 3 loaf pans with cooking spray and pour the dough into the bottom third of the pan. Let the dough rise in a warm place for about 3 hours, until it has risen above the edge of the pan.

Preheat the oven to 350°F. Bake on the center rack of the oven for 50 minutes, until golden brown. Immediately remove the bread from pans and let cool on a wire rack.

Servings	Calories	Protein	Carbohydrates	Fat
48	54	1 g	12 g	0 g

P i z z a

Pizza must be cooked on a stone or brick surface (see page 19) in a raging hot (550°F) oven. This is the only way you'll get an authentic crispy crust right in your own home!

Rather than give you a multitude of pizza recipes, I'm going to teach you the basics of pizza making so that you can create your own low-calorie, nutrient-rich pizzas. The nutritional values for most toppings can be found in the Nutritional Almanac (see page 219).

This dough can also be formed into a loaf to produce a very flavorful basic bread. Simply let it rise a second time and bake at 375°F until golden brown.

Pizza Crust

3 to 4 Tbs yellow cornmeal
1 sponge recipe (see recipe on page 185)
2 tsp salt
2 cups bread flour
olive-oil-flavored cooking spray

In the bowl of an electric mixer, combine the sponge, salt, and enough flour to make a soft wet dough. Using a paddle, beat the dough for 2 to 3 minutes on high speed. Reduce the speed to low and slowly add enough flour to make the dough pull away from the sides of the bowl and ball up around the paddle.

Turn the mixer off and scrape the dough back into the bowl with a rubber spatula. Replace the paddle with a dough hook and knead the dough for 3 to 5 minutes, adding just enough flour to keep it from sticking.

Knead for 3 to 5 minutes. Turn the dough out onto a lightly floured work surface and knead again for 3 or 4 turns. Shape the dough into a ball. Clean out the mixing bowl and coat it with olive-oil-flavored cooking spray. Roll the dough around inside the bowl to coat with the cooking spray. Cover the dough with plastic wrap and let rise in a warm place for 2 to 3 hours, until it has doubled in volume.

Preheat the oven to its highest setting (at least 550°F). Punch down the dough and turn it out onto a floured work surface. Knead the dough for 3 to 4 turns to coat with flour. Cut the dough into 12-ounce pieces and roll it out flat. Pick the round up and hold it between the thumb and fingers of each hand. Stretch and turn the dough in your hands until you have a thin circle, about 10 inches in diameter.

Lay the crust down on a wood peel than has been sprinkled with cornmeal. Gently shake the peel to make sure the dough isn't sticking. Add the toppings and bake.

Servings	Calories	Protein	Carbohydrates	Fat
8	231	6 g	50 g	1 g

Basic Pizza

12 oz pizza crust (see recipe page 188)

2/3 cup crushed tomatoes, canned

2 oz part-skim mozzarella cheese

1 Tbs grated Parmesan cheese

1 Tbs fresh basil, chopped

1/4 tsp salt

1/4 tsp black pepper

Preheat the oven to its highest setting (at least 550°F). Sprinkle the pizza peel liberally with cornmeal. Stretch the dough out, form the crust, and lay it on the peel.

Mix the basil with the tomatoes and spread the mixture evenly over the surface of the crust, leaving a 3/4-inch border around the edge. Evenly distribute the mozzarella over the sauce, and then sprinkle the Parmesan cheese over the mozzarella. Sprinkle the top with salt and pepper.

Open the oven door and carefully guide the pizza into the oven, holding the handle of the peel in one hand. Gently shake the peel to make sure that the pizza isn't sticking. Lay the peel on the bricks in the bottom of your oven. Quickly jerk the peel out from under the pizza, which should land on the bricks in the oven. Don't worry if you don't get it right the first time. Practice makes perfect!

Servings	Calories	Protein	Carbohydrates	Fat
8	265	8 g	53 g	1 g

Vege Fuel Bread

I have to give the credit for this recipe to my father, who inherited the job of making Vege Fuel Bread when I didn't have the patience to continue. After watching the birds outside my kitchen window chomp away on my third attempt, I knew it was time to call in a pro. For some reason, yeast-based breads react differently with Vege Fuel than baked goods that use baking powder to make them rise. My dad, the master baker, could make bread rise on the moon. I knew I needed his superior prowess if I was ever going to produce an edible loaf of Vege-Fuel-fortified bread.

Within a week, Dad called to tell me that he had come up with a solution: First, the ratio of flour to Vege Fuel must not exceed 3 to 1. Second, bran must be added to break up an otherwise gummy texture. In addition, Dad informed me that Federal Express would be dropping off a loaf at my house before 10:30 am the next morning.

He was true to his word. In record time, I was treated to a wonderful loaf of fresh, home-baked Vege Fuel bread. Although baking bread from scratch is no small task, it's certainly worth the effort. My father's recipe follows. Thanks, Dad.

Dad's Vege Fuel Bread

1 cup Vege Fuel

3 cups flour

1 1/2 cups bran

1/3 cup brown sugar

2 tsp salt

2 packages dry yeast

2 cups warm water (about 110°F)

cooking spray

In a very large mixing bowl, dissolve the brown sugar in the warm water. Add the yeast, stir, and set aside. In another bowl, combine the remaining ingredients. After a few minutes, the yeast will have bubbled up. Add it to the dry ingredients and mix well with the dough hook of an electric mixer. Either by hand or with the electric mixer, knead the dough until it has a firm, elastic consistency. Add small amounts of flour as needed to prevent sticking. Return the dough to a clean mixing bowl, cover with plastic wrap, and let rise in a warm place for about 3 hours, until it has doubled in volume.

Coat 2 loaf pans with cooking spray. Punch the dough down and scrape it out onto a floured work surface. Knead for 3 or 4 turns and divide it into 2 equal pieces. Place the pieces in the coated loaf pans. Cover with a towel and let the dough rise in a warm place for about 3 hours, until it has doubled in volume again.

Preheat the oven to 375°F. Bake until golden brown. Immediately remove the loaves from the pans and let cool on a wire rack.

Once the bread has cooled, slice the entire loaf or at least mark where each slice would go. If you don't, the bread will disappear before you can determine the nutritional content of each slice accurately. I was able to carve 16 slices per loaf.

Servings	Calories	Protein	Carbohydrates	Fat
32	82	6 g	34 g	0 g

Chapter Eleven

DESSERTS

Without a doubt, healthy dessert recipes are in high demand. The response to my TwinLab Muscle Meal Dessert series was amazing: I received no less than 700 letters a month! I'm still scratching my head trying to figure out why. I was never too interested in sweets, but it's obvious that I'm in the minority. Because the subject is so popular, I will one day devote an entire book to the subject of healthy desserts.

In the meantime, I hope the following recipes will hold you over. Just one word of caution: Although these recipes are pretty much devoid of fat and sugar, dessert should still come after your meal. It would bother me an awful lot if I found out that my readers were subsisting on cake.

Vanilla Custard

6 egg whites

1 cup non-fat milk

2 tsp vanilla

1 tsp cinnamon

1/2 tsp nutmeg

12 packets Sweet One sweetener*

cooking spray

Preheat the oven to 350°F. With a wire whisk, beat the egg whites with the sweetener until foamy and thick. Add the milk, vanilla, cinnamon, and nutmeg. Beat with a wire whisk until well blended

Coat 2 ramekins with cooking spray and pour in the mixture. Bake in a water bath (see page 25) for about 40 minutes, until set.

Servings	Calories	Protein	Carbohydrates	Fat
2	107	14 g	9 g	0 g

*Sweet One sweetener by Sunette is an artificial sweetener similar to Equal. The difference is that Sweet One stays sweet when cooked, while Equal turns bitter.

Espresso Custard

6 egg whites

1 cup non-fat milk

10 packets Sweet One sweetener

2 Tbs espresso

1/2 tsp nutmeg

cooking spray

Preheat the oven to 325°F. Slowly heat the milk in a non-stick saucepan. Just before it boils, remove it from the heat and add the coffee. Stir and set aside to steep.

With a wire whisk, beat the egg whites with the sweetener until foamy and thick. Whisk in the nutmeg until well blended.

Strain the espresso mixture through a cheesecloth-lined strainer into the egg whites, and whisk until well blended.

Coat 2 ramekins with cooking spray and pour in the mixture. Bake in a water bath (see page 25) for about 50 minutes, until set.

Servings	Calories	Protein	Carbohydrates	Fat
2	97	14 g	7 g	0 g

Blueberry Blintzes

16 oz low-fat cottage cheese

6 egg whites

10 packets Sweet One sweetener

3 Tbs cornstarch

2 tsp vanilla

1 tsp cinnamon

6 Tbs low-sugar blueberry preserves

cooking spray

Preheat the oven to 200°F. In a mixing bowl, beat the egg whites and the sweetener with a wire whisk until foamy and thick. Add the cottage cheese and cornstarch. Mix well. Add the vanilla and cinnamon and stir to incorporate.

Coat a small pan with cooking spray. Spread 1/6 of the mixture evenly over the bottom. Cover and cook over low heat for 3 to 4 minutes. Gently remove the blintz and place it on a plate. Keep each blintz warm in the oven while repeating the process 5 more times using the remaining mixture.

Spread 1 tablespoon of the preserves on half of each blintz, then roll up.

Servings	Calories	Protein	Carbohydrates	Fat
1 blintz	119	13 g	13 g	1 g

Apple Orange Raisin Chutney

1 apple, peeled, cored, quartered, and sliced

1/2 cup raisins

1 6 oz can of mandarin orange slices

1 Tbs honey

1 Tbs lime juice

1 tsp fresh mint, finely chopped

Mix the honey and lime juice together in a bowl with a wire whisk. Add the remaining ingredients and mix well.

Servings	Calories	Protein	Carbohydrates	Fat
16	31	0 g	6 g	0 g

Pumpkin Custard

2 lbs canned pumpkin

6 egg whites

24 packets Sweet One sweetener

3 tsp pumpkin spice

1/4 tsp salt

1 cup non-fat milk

2 tsp vanilla

cooking spray

Preheat the oven to 375°F. Beat the egg whites and the sweetener with a wire whisk until foamy and thick. Add the pumpkin spice and salt. Mix well. Add the milk and vanilla. Beat with a wire whisk until well blended.

Coat 4 ramekins with cooking spray and pour in the mixture. Bake in a water bath (see page 25) for about 1 hour, until set.

Servings	Calories	Protein	Carbohydrates	Fat
4	145	9 g	27 g	0 g

Chocolate Cake

3 egg whites

25 packets Sweet One sweetener

1 1/2 tsp vanilla

1 1/2 cups flour

1 1/2 Tbs baking soda

1 Tbs baking powder

1/3 cup non-fat yogurt

1/4 cup cocoa

1/4 tsp salt

1 3/4 cups water

2 tsp cinnamon

cooking spray

Preheat the oven to 325°F. In a mixing bowl, beat the egg whites, sweetener, and vanilla with a wire whisk until foamy and thick. Add the baking powder, yogurt, cocoa, salt, water, and cinnamon. Beat with a wire whisk until well blended.

Coat a 9-inch cake pan with cooking spray and pour in the batter. Bake for 35 minutes, until a toothpick inserted in the center comes out clean. Let cool on a wire rack.

Servings	Calories	Protein	Carbohydrates	Fat
8	133	7 g	24 g	1 g

Chocolate Icing

2 Tbs cocoa

1 tsp cornstarch

1 Tbs sweet rice flour

2 Tbs, more or less, non-fat milk

1 tsp vanilla

6 packets Equal sweetener

Mix the dry ingredients in a small bowl. In another bowl, pour the vanilla into the milk. Stirring the dry mixture constantly with a wire whisk, add just enough of the milk and vanilla mixture to form the icing. If the icing is too stiff, stir in small amounts of milk until it has the desired consistency.

Servings	Calories	Protein	Carbohydrates	Fat
8	13	1 g	2 g	0 g

Fat-Free Sugar-Free Chocolate Cheesecake

32 oz fat-free cottage cheese

3 envelopes of unflavored gelatin

3/4 cup water

25 packets of Equal sweetener

1 cup non-fat sour cream

3 Tbs cocoa

1 tsp cinnamon

Crust

1 cup Honey Graham Cereal

1 tsp cinnamon

3 packets Equal sweetener

<u>Crust</u>

In a food processor or blender, grind the ingredients to the consistency of coarse meal. Spread evenly over the bottom of a cheesecake pan.

<u>Cheesecake</u>

Dissolve the gelatin in 3/4 cup of water. Let stand for 2 minutes, then microwave for 40 seconds. Stir and set aside.

Combine the cottage cheese, 2/3 of the heated gelatin, and the 20 packets of sweetener in the food processor. Blend until smooth, then pour into a mixing bowl. Combine the sour cream, vanilla, cinnamon, 5 packets of sweetener, cocoa, and remaining gelatin in the food processor and blend until smooth. Add to the cheese mixture. Mix with an electric mixer for about 2 minutes.

Gently pour the mixture onto the crust in the cheesecake pan. Cover with plastic wrap and refrigerate overnight.

Servings	Calories	Protein	Carbohydrates	Fat
8	139	19 g	11 g	1 g

Poached Pears in Raspberry Sauce

2 cups water

2 cups red wine

2 cups raspberries

1 plus 1/2 cups frozen apple juice concentrate

4 pears

1/2-inch slice of ginger

1 tsp cinnamon

1 tsp nutmeg

1 Tbs cornstarch

1/4 cup water

Carefully peel and core the pears, making sure to leave the stems attached. Trim the bottom of the pears flat so that the pears stand up straight.

Combine the red wine, water, 1 cup apple juice concentrate, cinnamon, nutmeg, ginger, and raspberries (reserve a few for garnishing) in a saucepan. Bring to a boil. Add the pears and lower the heat. Cover and poach for 30 to 40 minutes, until a knife can easily be inserted into the bottom of the pear at its thickest point.

Remove the pears and set aside. Add the remaining apple juice concentrate to the saucepan and bring back to a boil. Reduce the liquid by half. Dissolve the cornstarch in 1/4 cup of water. Remove the pan from the heat and stir the cornstarch mixture into the sauce until thickened. Strain and refrigerate.

To serve, place each pear in the center of a dessert plate. Pour 1/4 cup of sauce over each pear and garnish with extra raspberries.

Servings	Calories	Protein	Carbohydrates	Fat
4	213	4 g	52 g	1 g

Rice Pudding

1 cup long-grain white rice

4 cups non-fat milk

3 Tbs oatmeal powder

1 tsp nutmeg

2 Tbs cinnamon

1/2 cup raisins

25 packets Equal sweetener

1 Tbs vanilla

Combine the rice, oatmeal powder, milk, and raisins in a 2-quart saucepan and bring to a boil. Reduce the heat to low. Cover and cook for 20 to 30 minutes, until the rice is very tender and the liquid has thickened. Remove from the heat, cover, and let stand for 20 minutes.

Stir in the nutmeg, cinnamon, and Equal until well-blended. Pour the mixture into a 9- by 13-inch baking dish and sprinkle the top with more cinnamon. Cover with plastic wrap and refrigerate overnight.

Servings	Calories	Protein	Carbohydrates	Fat
8	119	5 g	22 g	1 g

Boston Cream Pie

1 chocolate cake (see recipe on page 201)
1 chocolate icing (see recipe on page 202)
1 package instant non-fat vanilla pudding made with non-fat milk

Split the cake with a long slicing knife. Spread the prepared pudding evenly over the bottom half of the cake. Carefully place the top half on top of the pudding and spread the icing over the entire cake.

Servings	Calories	Protein	Carbohydrates	Fat
8	152	8 g	27 g	1 g

Frozen Yogurt

32 oz non-fat plain yogurt
1/2 cup sugar-free fruit spread
12 packets Equal sweetener

Combine the ingredients in a bowl and mix thoroughly. Pour the mixture into a bowl, cover with plastic wrap, and refrigerate for at least 2 hours. Process according to your ice cream maker's directions. Divide the finished product into 4 separate containers and store in the freezer.

Servings	Calories	Protein	Carbohydrates	Fat
4	158	11 g	29 g	0 g

Yam Pie

3 cups cooked, skinned yam

8 packets Sweet One sweetener

3 egg whites

1 tsp cinnamon

1/2 tsp cloves

Crust

1 1/2 cups Golden Graham cereal

cooking spray

Crust

Preheat the oven to 325°F. In a food processor or blender, grind the cereal to the consistency of coarse meal. Coat a pie tin with cooking spray and add the ground cereal, pushing it up the sides to form a crust.

Filling

Combine the yam, sweetener, egg whites, cinnamon, and cloves in a bowl. Mix well with a fork, mashing the mixture through the tines until smooth. Pour the mixture onto the pie crust in the pie tin. Spread the mixture across the bottom gently, taking care not to disturb the crust. Bake for about 40 minutes, until set. Cool and serve.

Servings	Calories	Protein	Carbohydrates	Fat
6	109	3 g	25 g	0 g

Chocolate Ice Cream

1 can Carnation Light evaporated skim milk

4 egg whites

12 packets Equal sweetener

1/3 cup cocoa

1 cup non-fat milk

Combine all of the ingredients in a blender and pulse until smooth. Pour the mixture into a bowl, cover with plastic wrap, and refrigerate for at least 2 hours. Process according to your ice cream maker's directions. Divide the finished product into 4 separate containers and store in the freezer.

Servings	Calories	Protein	Carbohydrates	Fat
4	152	11 g	13 g	6 g

Vanilla Ice Cream

1 can Carnation Light evaporated skim milk

4 egg whites

12 packets Equal sweetener

2 vanilla beans

1 cup non-fat milk

Bring the evaporated and non-fat milk to a boil in a small saucepan. Add the vanilla beans. Remove from the heat and cover. Let the vanilla beans steep for 2 hours.

Retrieve the vanilla beans from the pot and split lengthwise with a sharp knife. Open the beans and use a spoon to scrape the contents into the milk. Discard the empty pods.

Pour the milk and vanilla mixture into a blender. Add the egg whites and sweetener. Pulse several times, taking care not to kick up too much foam. Pour the mixture into a bowl, cover with plastic wrap, and refrigerate for at least 2 hours.

Process the mixture according to your ice cream maker's directions. Divide the finished product into 4 separate containers and store in the freezer.

Servings	Calories	Protein	Carbohydrates	Fat
4	127	10 g	10 g	5 g

You can create many variations using this vanilla ice cream as a base. For example, try adding 1/2 cup stale chocolate cake crumbs (see recipe on page 201) during the final stages of processing. Chopped fruit, granola—anything you can think of—can be added. Just keep track of the nutritional content of whatever you add so that you can adjust the total.

Vege-Fuel-Fortified Desserts

Vege-Fuel-fortified desserts make it possible for you to eat your cake and have a hard body too! While you should not consider them your main course, Vege-Fuel-fortified desserts contain a powerful amount of quality protein. If you have a sweet-tooth, these desserts will satisfy your cravings—without guilt!

Packaged Cake Mixes

It is now possible to get your protein from cake! Vege Fuel can be added to any packaged cake mix simply by measuring the amount of cake mix in the box and adding half that amount of Vege Fuel to the dry mix. Follow the recipe on the box, increasing the liquid to account for the extra powder. Add additional sweetener to taste and 1 teaspoon of baking powder for each 1/2 cup of mix.

Although packaged cake mix is convenient, you can easily make protein-fortified desserts from scratch. The following recipes contain no sugar or fat! Do I have your attention?

Vege Fuel Chocolate Cake

1 cup all-purpose flour
4 scoops Vege Fuel
1/2 tsp salt
1/3 cup cocoa
1 Tbs baking powder
3 egg whites
12 packets Sweet One sweetener
1 cup non-fat milk
cooking spray

Preheat the oven to 350°F. Combine the dry ingredients in a bowl and mix well. In another bowl, beat the milk and the egg whites with a wire whisk. Add the milk and egg whites to the dry ingredients. Quickly beat the mixture until well blended (a few small lumps are okay). If the batter seems a little too stiff, add some milk.

Coat a 9-inch cake pan with cooking spray and pour in the batter. Bake for about

30 minutes, until a toothpick inserted into the center comes out clean. Let cool on a wire rack.

Servings	Calories	Protein	Carbohydrates	Fat
8	133	16 g	15 g	1 g

Vege Fuel Angel Food Cake

8 egg whites

1 cup all-purpose flour

2 tsp baking powder

4 scoops Vege Fuel

1 cup non-fat milk

15 packets Sweet One sweetener

2 Tbs vanilla extract

1/2 tsp salt

cooking spray

Preheat the oven to 350°F. Combine the dry ingredients in a bowl and mix well. Add the milk and vanilla. Mix with a wire whisk until well blended.

In another bowl, beat the egg whites to stiff peaks. Mix 1/4 of the beaten egg whites into the cake batter, then fold in the remaining egg whites. Work quickly to prevent deflating the egg whites.

Coat a 9-inch cake pan with cooking spray and pour in the batter. Bake for 40 minutes, until a toothpick inserted into the center comes out clean. Let cool on a wire rack.

Servings	Calories	Protein	Carbohydrates	Fat
8	135	18 g	14 g	0 g

Chocolate Icing

1/3 cup cocoa

1 scoop Vege Fuel

8 packets Equal sweetener

1 tsp vanilla extract

1/4 cup non-fat milk

Mix the dry ingredients in a small bowl. In another bowl, pour the vanilla into the milk. Stirring the dry mixture constantly with a wire whisk, add just enough of the milk and vanilla mixture to form the icing. If the icing is too stiff, stir in small amounts of milk until it has the desired consistency.

Servings	Calories	Protein	Carbohydrates	Fat
8	31	4 g	2 g	1 g

Vege Fuel Rice Pudding

1 cup white rice

4 scoops Vege Fuel

1 quart non-fat milk

12 packets Equal sweetener

2 tsp cinnamon

1 tsp nutmeg

2 Tbs vanilla extract

Using a blender, dissolve the Vege Fuel in the milk. Combine this mixture with the rice in a 2-quart saucepan. Slowly bring the mixture to a boil, stirring constantly. As the mixture begins to boil, reduce the heat to low. Cover and cook for 20 to 30 minutes, until the rice is very tender and the liquid has thickened.

Remove from the heat and stir in the cinnamon, nutmeg, sweetener, and vanilla. Pour the mixture into a 9- by 13-inch baking dish and sprinkle the top with more cinnamon. Cover with plastic wrap and refrigerate overnight.

Servings	Calories	Protein	Carbohydrates	Fat
8	131	17 g	14 g	0 g

Vege Fuel Vanilla Custard

6 egg whites

1 cup non-fat milk

2 scoops Vege Fuel

6 packets Sweet One sweetener

2 Tbs vanilla extract

1/4 tsp ground nutmeg

Preheat the oven to 325°F. Combine the ingredients in a blender and pulse just enough to dissolve any lumps. Pour the mixture into a small aluminum loaf pan.

Bake the custard in a water bath (see page 25) for 1 hour and 15 minutes or until firm. Let cool, then refrigerate. Serve cold.

This dish contains a tremendous amount of complete protein and tastes nothing like protein powder! You can make several of them at one time and keep them in the refrigerator for a few days. How many? Don't ask me——I eat them too fast.

Servings	Calories	Protein	Carbohydrates	Fat
4	111	19 g	5 g	0 g

Vege Fuel Chocolate Ice Cream

1 can Carnation Light evaporated skim milk

4 egg whites

12 packets Equal sweetener

1/3 cup cocoa

3 scoops Vege Fuel

Combine all of the ingredients in a blender. Pulse until smooth. Pour the mixture into a bowl, cover with plastic wrap, and refrigerate for at least 2 hours.

Process according to your ice cream maker's directions. Divide the finished product into 4 separate containers and store in the freezer.

Servings	Calories	Protein	Carbohydrates	Fat
4	205	27 g	11 g	6 g

Vege Fuel Vanilla Ice Cream

1 can Carnation Light evaporated skim milk

4 egg whites

12 packets Equal sweetener

2 vanilla beans

3 scoops Vege Fuel

Bring the evaporated milk to a boil in a small saucepan. Add the vanilla beans. Remove from the heat and cover. Let the vanilla beans steep for 2 hours.

Retrieve the vanilla beans from the pan and split lengthwise with a sharp knife. Open the beans and use a spoon to scrape the contents into the milk. Discard the empty pods.

Pour the milk and vanilla mixture into a blender and add the egg whites, sweetener, and Vege Fuel. Pulse several times, taking care not to kick up too much foam. Pour the mixture into a bowl, cover with plastic wrap, and refrigerate for at least 2 hours.

Process the mixture according to your ice cream maker's directions. Divide the finished product into 4 separate containers and store in the freezer.

Servings	Calories	Protein	Carbohydrates	Fat
4	180	25 g	8 g	5 g

You can create many variations using this vanilla ice cream as a base. For example, try adding 1/2 cup stale chocolate cake crumbs (see recipe on page 201) during the final stages of processing. Chopped fruit, granola——anything you can think of——can be added. Just keep track of the nutritional content of whatever you add so that you can adjust the total.

Vege Fuel Strawberry Frozen Yogurt

32 oz non-fat plain yogurt
2 scoops Vege Fuel
10 packets Equal sweetener
6 oz (1/2 jar) Smucker's light sugar-free strawberry fruit spread

Divide the yogurt in half and place each half into a fine strainer suspended over a bowl. Cover with plastic wrap and refrigerate for 24 hours. The only way to fortify the yogurt with Vege Fuel is to separate the liquid (the whey), mix the Vege Fuel with the whey, and then add the whey back to the solids. Be sure to mix vigorously with a wire whisk.)

Add the strawberry fruit spread and the sweetener to the fortified yogurt, cover, and refrigerate for at least 2 hours. Process the yogurt according to your ice cream maker's directions. Divide the finished product into 4 separate containers and store in the freezer.

Servings	Calories	Protein	Carbohydrates	Fat
4	274	23 g	45 g	0 g

You can substitute any flavor of sugar-free fruit spread. Or, try adding 1/3 cup of cocoa and another 5 packets of Equal to make chocolate yogurt. Just keep track of the nutritional content of whatever you add so that you can adjust the total. Extracts, such as vanilla or almond, or spices, like nutmeg or cinnamon, can also be added without adding any calories. You may even want to try serving frozen yogurt with one of the cake recipes for a truly decadent, super high-protein dessert. Be creative and enjoy.

Chapter Twelve

NUTRITIONAL ALMANAC

Vegetables

Serving	Food	Calories	Protein	Carbohydrate	Fat
1	Artichoke	53	3 g	12 g	0 g
1 cup	Asparagus	44	5 g	8 g	1 g
1 oz	Avocado	36	1 g	2 g	3 g
1	Beets	52	2 g	11 g	0 g
1 cup	Broccoli	46	5 g	9 g	0 g
2 cups	Cabbage (raw)	32	2 g	8 g	1 g
1	Carrot	31	1 g	7 g	0 g
6 stalks	Celery	36	2 g	9 g	1 g
2 cups	Cucumber	28	0 g	6 g	0 g
1 cup	Eggplant	26	1 g	6 g	0 g
1	Green beans	44	2 g	10 g	0 g
1 cup	Kale (cooked)	43	5 g	7 g	1 g
3 cups	Lettuce	30	2 g	7 g	0 g
1 cup	Mushrooms (raw)	20	2 g	3 g	0 g
1/2 cup	Onions	27	1 g	6 g	0 g
1/2 cup	Peas (cooked)	59	4 g	11 g	0 g
2 cups	Spinach	24	3 g	4 g	0 g
1 cup	Squash, summer (cooked)	36	2 g	8 g	1 g
1/2 cup	Squash, winter (cooked)	39	1 g	9 g	1 g
1 cup	Swiss chard (cooked)	36	3 g	7 g	0 g
1	Tomato	34	2 g	8 g	0 g
1/2 cup	Tomato Sauce	54	2 g	12 g	0 g
2 cups	Zucchini	36	3 g	8 g	0 g

F r u i t s

Serving	Food	Calories	Protein	Carbohydrate	Fat
1/2 apple	Apple	40	0 g	12 g	0 g
3	Apricot	51	2 g	12 g	0 g
1/2 of one	Banana	53	1 g	13 g	0 g
1/2 cup	Blackberries	37	1 g	9 g	0 g
1/2 cup	Blueberries	41	1 g	10 g	0 g
1/2 of one	Cantaloupe	94	2 g	22 g	1 g
1/2 cup	Cherries	52	1 g	12 g	1 g
1/2 of one	Grapefruit	41	1 g	11 g	0 g
1/2 cup	Grapes	57	1 g	14 g	0 g
1/2 of one	Nectarine	34	0 g	8 g	0 g
1	Orange	62	1 g	15 g	0 g
1	Peach	38	1 g	10 g	1 g
1 cup	Pineapple	77	1 g	19 g	1 g
2 plums	Plums	72	1 g	18 g	1 g
1 cup	Raspberries	61	1 g	14 g	1 g
1 cup	Strawberries	45	1 g	10 g	1 g
1 cup	Watermelon	50	1 g	12 g	0 g

Grains

Serving	Food	Calories	Protein	Carbohydrate	Fat
1/2 of one	Bagel	74	3 g	14 g	1 g
1 slice	Bread, whole wheat	61	2 g	11 g	1 g
1/2 ear	Corn on the cob	80	2 g	16 g	0 g
1 piece	Cornbread	93	3 g	13 g	3 g
1 oz	Cream of wheat	100	3 g	22 g	0 g
3 oz	Garbanzo Beans	71	4 g	12 g	1 g
1 oz	Grape Nuts	110	3 g	23 g	0 g
1/2 cup	Lentils (cooked)	115	9 g	20 g	0 g
1/2 of one	Muffin	56	2 g	9 g	2 g
1/2 cup	Oatmeal (cooked)	66	2 g	12 g	1 g
1/2 cup	Pasta	100	3 g	20 g	0 g
1 cup	Popcorn	54	2 g	11 g	1 g
1/2 of one	Potato (baked)	110	2 g	26 g	0 g
1/2 cup	Rice	100	2 g	25 g	0 g
2	Rice cakes	70	1 g	16 g	0 g
1/2 cup	Shredded wheat	68	2 g	17 g	0 g
3 oz	Yams	90	2 g	21 g	0 g

Protein

Serving	Food	Calories	Protein	Carbohydrate	Fat
4 oz	Bass	118	21 g	0 g	2 g
4 oz	Carp	144	20 g	0 g	6 g
4 oz	Catfish	132	21 g	0 g	5 g
4 slices	Cheese (fat-free)	120	18 g	12 g	0 g
3 oz	Chicken breast (baked)	123	21 g	0 g	5 g
6 oz	Clams	126	21 g	4 g	2 g
5 oz	Cod	111	25 g	0 g	1 g
4 oz	Cottage cheese (fat-free)	105	23 g	5 g	0 g
7	Egg whites	119	25 g	2 g	0 g
5 oz	Haddock	123	26 g	0 g	1 g
3 oz	Halibut	119	23 g	0 g	3 g
2 oz	Lamb	125	15 g	0 g	7 g
1 1/2 cups	Milk (non-fat)	129	12 g	18 g	1 g
6 oz	Oysters	138	16 g	8 g	4 g
4 oz	Red snapper	106	23 g	0 g	1 g
3 oz	Salmon	121	17 g	0 g	5 g
5 oz	Scallops	115	22 g	5 g	0 g
15	Shrimp	113	22 g	1 g	2 g
6 oz	Sole	117	26 g	0 g	1 g
2 oz	Steak	138	15 g	0 g	9 g
4 oz	Tuna	140	30 g	0 g	2 g
2 oz	Turkey breast	104	21 g	0 g	2 g
3 oz	Whitefish	114	16 g	0 g	5 g
8 oz	Yogurt (non-fat)	127	13 g	17 g	0 g

Condiments

Serving	*Food*	*Calories*	*Protein*	*Carbohydrate*	*Fat*
2 Tbs	Catsup	32	1 g	8 g	0 g
1 Tbs	Honey	64	0 g	17 g	0 g
1 Tsp	Mustard	5	<1 g	<1 g	0 g
1/2 cup	Salsa	30	0 g	8 g	0 g
6 Tbs	Sour cream (non-fat)	54	6 g	9 g	0 g

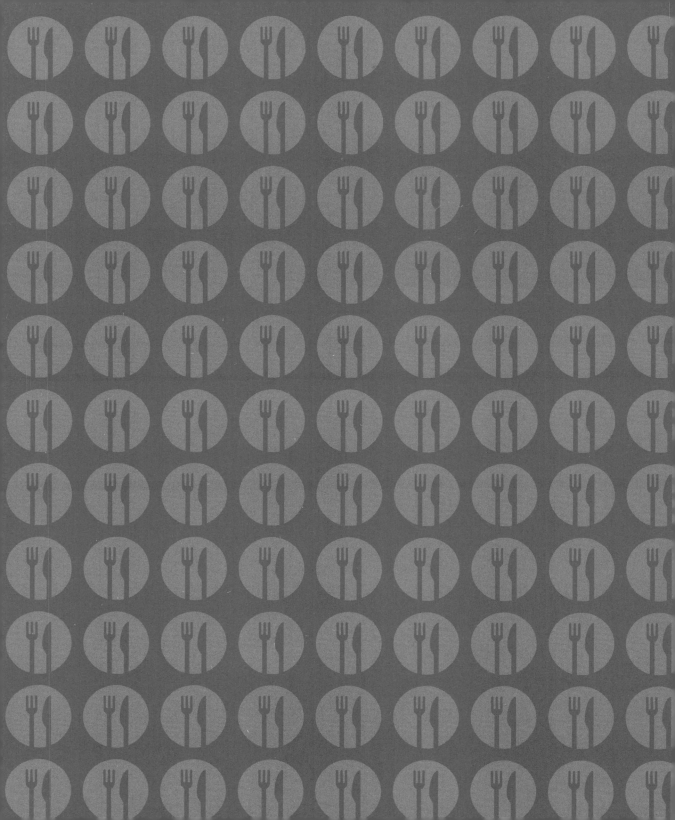